Writing Free

Writing Free

edited by

Irene Staunton

WEAVER
PRESS

Published by Weaver Press, Box A1922, Avondale, Harare. 2011
<www.weaverpresszimbabwe.com>

'Miss McConkey of Bridgewater Close' by Petina Gappah was first
published in the *Guardian* in 2009. We are grateful for permission to
reproduce it here.

Typeset by Weaver Press
Cover Design: Danes Design, Harare
Printed by: Benaby Printing and Publishing, Harare

ISBN: 978-1-77922-157-5

Contents

'Writing free' … words that perhaps offer a small provocation, a small challenge to writers to extend their boundaries, to think something through from a lateral perspective, to approach a topic differently, to turn a persepctive inside out. Good writing searches beneath superficial exteriors, seeks for insights that resonate, reaches beyond the known, the clichéd, the tendency to evade what is hard to confront.

In this collection, each writer helps us to explore and appreciate an idea anew. As Anaïs Nin aptly wrote, 'The role of a writer is not to say what we all can say, but what we are unable to say'.

Freedom is something that we often don't realise we possess, until it is taken away.

Irene Staunton

Authors' biographies and commentaries on Writing Free

Jonathon Brakarsh is a health professional and writer who moved to Zimbabwe in 1993. He began his career working in the off-off-Broadway theatre district in New York City as a playwright and stage manager. Zimbabwe is a continuous source of inspiration for his stories as each day presents challenges which Zimbabweans face with grace, resilience and ingenuity.

'Running in Zimbabwe' was inspired by the announcement from Irene Staunton, seeking contributions to Weaver Press's anthology Writing Free. After reading her e-mail, three stories, which had been sitting in my mind, suddenly started coalescing, fighting for places in the larger narrative. Being given the opportunity to 'write free' was an offer I could not refuse. So, I spent an intense period of time writing and revising. What emerged was a story about the desire most people have for freedom, and how the oppression present in Zimbabwe insinuates itself into every action of life. Love, a sense of belonging and the social fabric which bonds neighbours and relatives together can dilute the poisons that have mixed into the motion of our daily lives. How we obtain our vision of freedom continues to be discovered. This story puts these issues on the table using black humour, irony and a hope for change. Thanks to my son, Sam, for suggesting an ending to this story, which until recently was in search of itself.

Petina Gappah is the author of *An Elegy for Easterly* (2009), a collection of short stories which was awarded the Guardian First Book Award and short-listed for the Orwell Book Prize, the Los Angeles Times First Book Award, the Frank O'Connor Short Story Award and Zimbabwe's National Arts Merit Award. It has been published in more than a dozen languages. Taking a sabbatical break from her career as an international trade lawyer in Geneva, Petina currently lives in Harare, from where she writes, travels and chairs the Board of the Harare City Library. Her first novel will be published in 2012.

At the heart of my story, 'Miss McConkey of Bridgewater Close', is an explo-

ration of the social burdens that came with Zimbabwe's freedom, with its independence, particularly the burdens borne by the black children who were the first to go to formerly 'whites only' schools and thus integrated these schools. I was one of those children. The sharpest memory I have of those days is the constant fear that I had done or said something wrong, something that would expose me to the stares and humiliating comments of my classmates. While the nation was celebrating its independence, while black parents were celebrating the opening up of educational opportunities that had been closed to their children, these same children were experiencing freedom as agony. However, my story is also about another kind of being free, it is about the freedom that comes from forgiveness, the freedom that comes with letting go of the memory of pain.

Tendai Huchu, author of the *Hairdresser of Harare* was born in Bindura, Zimbabwe. He has a great love of literature, and currently lives in Edinburgh, Scotland.

My first thought when I was asked to submit a short story for Writing Free was, 'I'm not getting paid for this am I?'
The 'Writing' part was easy to understand but the 'Free' left so much breadth for imagination – an artistic licence to create anything at all. In imagining 'Crossroads' I fused childhood memories with fiction and borrowed styles from authors I admire. I thought the narrative of a man bound to his wife and job in a foreign country reminiscing on his careFree childhood would fit well in the anthology, but if you look at the story closely, even this idealised childhood has subtle limitations imposed upon it.

Ethel Irene Kabwato was born in Mutare, Zimbabwe into a creative family and has a BA in Media Studies from the Zimbabwe Open University. She participated in the British Council Crossing Borders Project in 2004 and has had her poetry published in the anthology *Sunflowers in your Eyes*. Currently, she is working on a project called Slum Cinema, a voluntary initiative that seeks to empower disadvantaged communities through multimedia work. Her inspiration is derived from her two daughters, Nadia and Wynona.

'Footprints of Time' is a story set in rural Zimbabwe after the inception of the Government of National Unity. The story explores the theme of migration and *how it has affected some Zimbabwean families. My story can be defined as 'writing free' because it centres on the disturbances that rocked the country after the disputed March 29 elections in 2008, and the choices that people made in response to the situation. In this case, the main character, Steve, who is now based in the United Kingdom, struggles to come to terms with the death of his wife, Hannah, whom he abandoned after she had been gang-raped.*

Donna Kirstein was born in 1985. Raised in Zimbabwe, she has led a fairly nomadic life, growing up in various towns and farms during which she developed a passion for reading. She has always harboured a secret desire to write and she has recently been fortunate enough to study towards a joint degree in Fine Art, English and Creative Writing at the University of Chichester in the UK. She intends to continue travelling and to return home to Zimbabwe one day soon.

'The Situation' is an experimental short story that stems from the frustration of reading and watching the news about the problems in Zimbabwe. In writing the story, I was strongly influenced by news stories about the crisis. My story offers four voices: the three voices in the main section are fragmented, and can be read individually or in varying combinations. The concept is that no single voice can be wholly right or wholly wrong. 'The Situation' was inspired by newspaper articles but takes as its starting point the resilience of Zimbabweans.
'Writing Free' is a positive concept, and can be seen as a celebration of the will to survive and adaptability of Zimbabweans in the face of difficulty. Both 'The Situation' and 'Writing Free' represent writing with the freedom of individual voices and writing a way into a new future; the concept allows for self-determination, regardless of style, genre or ideas. It's about moving forward with hope for the future.

Ignatius Tirivangani Mabasa is a writer and storyteller who primarily writes in Shona. Although now well-known as a poet and novelist, Ignatius says, 'I started telling stories before I could write, re-telling the stories my grandmother told me, and adding new twists to the plot. You could say that this was the process by which I became a creative writer.' He has published two novels to date: *Ndafa Here?* and *Mapenzi* both of which have won local awards, and he has poems and short stories published on various websites. In 2010, Ignatius was the writer and storyteller in residence at the

Centre for Creative Writing and Oral Culture at the University of Manitoba in Canada for three and half months.

'The Novel Citizen' is an almost bizarre, multi-layered, metaphorical story, that attempts to explore certain thought processes in the life of a writer and the art of writing using madness as a device. What makes this story exciting to me is how it is being told by a vagrant who invites the listener to be an active participant and finish the story for him when he gets murdered by the real writer of the story. Yet, there is the question, who owns the story? Who is the teller of the story? What is the role of a writer and how 'alive' do the characters in a novel become?
The novel, through this story, is a contested area and readers and characters are not passive.

Daniel Mandishona is an architect. He was born in Harare in 1959 and brought up by his maternal grandparents in Mbare (then known as Harari township). In 1976 he was expelled from Goromonzi Secondary School and lived in London from 1977-92. He first studied Graphic Design then Architecture at the Bartlett School, University College London. He now has his own architectural practice in Harare. His short stories have been published in various anthologies, and he has his own published collection in *White Gods, Black Demons*.

'Freedom without sacrifice is like a mirage in the desert...'
George's domestic problems with his pregnant wife Helen stem from his womanising and late nights. His entire existence has led to one calamity after another. One night, after yet another bruising war of words with his wife, he storms off into the night to drink off his frustrations at his usual haunts. His aimless meanderings through the city centre eventually lead him to a crowded bar where he meets Sophie, one of his numerous paramours. It is only when George returns to her dingy lodgings that his conscience finally gets the better of him. In a self-liberating act he flees naked into the night, finally realising that his fate is not at the mercy of the gods but lies firmly in his own hands.

Isabella Matambanadzo (Ms.) is a Zimbabwean feminist. Born in 1973, she was raised with a deep awareness of her country's struggles for liberation and self-determination, which has influenced her life's path. Her love for the arts won her a prestigious Reuters Foundation scholarship to study

Journalism, Literature and Theatre Studies at Rhodes University in Grahamstown. In addition to working on the campus newspaper, serving on the founding team of the Cue TV, the Grahamstown Arts Festival television channel, and broadcasting on the campus radio station RMR, she supported herself by working as a waitress and reading audio books at a centre for the blind. She graduated with triple majors, Summa cum Laude and achieved Dean's List recognition and Academic Colours in 1999. Isabella enjoys reading, writing, painting, gardening and making jewellry.

My story, 'The Missing', focuses on a couple's romantic reminiscences which are disrupted by an unexpected, yet common event. Set in a country where ghosts still live, this is an intimate story about children in search of their mysterious past. A truth they can never quite know, or discover. A truth that cannot be laid to a peaceful rest but one that will certainly set them free.

No Violet Mkha from Bulawayo is currenty living in the United States. She recently received an MFA from Cornell University and is completing work on a novel. Her short story 'Hitting Budapest' won the Caine Prize, 2011.

'Shamisos' was written from a space of freedom that as a writer I find both gratifying and dizzying; especially now, knowing what I know about the experiences of some artists in places – which do not need mentioning – where they cannot freely express themselves. To me, therefore, 'writing free' means that I am telling the story that I want and choose to tell, in my truest voice, and on my own terms. This is where I am now, no matter what happens.

Christopher Mlalazi is the Nordic Africa Institute 2011 Guest Writer in Uppsala Sweden. In 2010 he was the Villa Aurora Guest Writer in Los Angeles, USA. Prolific as a prose writer and playwright, in 2008 he was the co-winner of the Oxfam Novib PEN Freedom of Expression Award at the Hague for theatre, and in 2009 was awarded a NAMA award for his short story collection, *Dancing With Life:Tales From The Township*. He was nominated for another NAMA for his 2009 novel, *Many Rivers*. In 2010 he won a NAMA for his play *Election Day*, which played to full houses. He has also published short stories extensively both in Zimbabwe and internationally. His latest play, *Colours of Dreams*, also opened to a full house at the Harare International Festival of the Arts in 2011.

The concept 'Writing Free' is the embodiment of the divine search to extend the creative process into realms where there are no boundaries, where taboos are scrutinised and cast aside, and where all forms of mental fetter, be they inhuman or humane (some humane acts can be retrogressive) are reduced to one big comic act. A world that writes, talks, plays and competes freely is a blessing that can only enrich our lives.

Blessing Musariri s a published and award-winning author with two childen's books to date, *Rufaro's Day* and *Going Home: A Tree's Story*. Her poetry has been published in *Sunflowers in your Eyes* and on the Poetry International website, as well as in various anthologies. Her short stories have been published in *African Love Stories* and in *Women Writing Zimbabwe*. She currently resides in Zimbabwe but treasures opportunities to travel within Africa and experience different local cultures. She mistakenly believed she would be a lawyer but came to her senses after sitting and passing the English Bar Finals in 1997. Blessing also holds an MA in Diplomatic Studies from the University of Westminster.

'The truth shall set you free.'
The promise of freedom to experiment opened me up to a new kind of story, a different narrative construction. In the same way, in his last hours, the main character feels the freedom to try methods other than the conventional, to discover the truth of something that bothered him until his dying day, including, at last, freeing his mind from the constructs of his religion to believe that he is about to commune with the spirit of a dead girl.
The story also addresses the assumption that death will grant us freedom from all the things that trouble us in life.

Ambrose Musiyiwa is a law student at De Montfort University in Leicester, and has worked as a teacher and a journalist. One of his short stories was featured in *Writing Now* while others have appeared in magazines that include *Tripod* (Literature Network, Leicester) and *African Writing Online*. He facilitates the blog, Conversations with Writers, which presents interviews with writers, publishers and literary activists from all over the world.

I believe that 'Danfo Driver' fits into the concept of 'writing free' because the story is told exclusively from the point of view of the child, Danny. As the story

develops we begin to see how the little boy tries to cope with the harsh reality of his life by increasingly relying on his own imagination as a way of coping and a means of escape.

I hope the impression the reader is left with is that of a child who just might turn out all right, notwithstanding the very difficult circumstances under which he is living – or rather surviving.

Sekai Nyenya is a writer and an international development consultant specialising in NGO accountability, health, microenterprise and human rights. She was born in rural Zimbabwe and trained as a nurse at Great Ormond Street in London. She holds a Ph.D. in International Relations from the University of Melbourne, Australia. Her essays, fiction and short stories have been published in a number of journals including the UK *Guardian Weekly*. Her second novel, *Songs to an African Sunset, a Zimbabwean Story*, presents stories of everyday life and the challenges of poverty in rural Zimbabwe. After 25 years working in humanitarian aid in Australia, Africa and the United States, Sekai returned to Zimbabwe in 2010. Confronted with the consequences of HIV/AIDS and increasing deaths and poverty in her village, she and the Village Women's Burial Society formed the Simukai Development Project whose aim is to seek practical sustainable solutions to solving rural poverty. At the same time, the project reclaims the voices of marginalised village communities through song, dance, writing and drama.

'The Donor's Visit' represents the 'free' voice of a grandmother in Zimbabwe today. The story explores the nature of power and the cultural dynamics between donors and the beneficiaries. The grandmother is free to speak her mind regarding her truth in relation to Zimbabwe's past, and to express her feeling about the present and its supposed value systems.

Fungisayi Sasa says that she has 'always had a passion for writing and reading' but it was when she moved to England that she realised that she could turn a hobby into a career. When she writes she feels she is 'paying homage to all the people in my life who introduced me to fiction and writing. They showed me that my reality does not have to be limited to the here and now but it can also be a journey through the imaginary'. Her poetry has been published on Poetry International website and her first children's book, *The Search for the Perfect Head*, is available on Amazon. She is currently working on a second children's book and a collection of short stories.

Free, freedom, freedom of speech. These were all words I took for granted until I came to England and watched from afar as the liberty of my countrymen was trampled on. I was safe here; I can speak from here. Though I could have written a political piece, bewailing the tattered state of my country, I decided to tackle an altogether different subject. The story itself is not political but the title definitely is. The phrase 'Turn Your Eyes On Me', is a cry for acknowledgement, a call to be noticed. It is the shriek of a woman whose husband has locked her out of their house and kept all her belongings, all her children. We are all locked out of the promises independence was supposed to bring us, tossed out, whispering to anyone who will hear, 'Turn your eyes on, turn your eyes on me.' I am writing free.

Emmanuel Sigauke grew up in Zvishavane, Zimbabwe, where he started writing at the age of thirteen. He teaches composition, literature and creative writing at Cosumnes River College in Sacramento, is a board member of the Sacramento Poetry Center, hosts poetry readings, is the book review editor of the organisation's bi-monthly newsletter, and is also the co-editor of the recently published *African Roar: An Eclectic Collection of African Authors*. Sigauke has also taught fiction workshops for the UC Davis Extension and the Hart Senior Center Annual Writing Conference. His fiction and poetry have appeared in literary journals and anthologies

This story freed me creatively as it is a departure from the issues which I have often dealt with before: stories set in the places of my childhood, recreating memorable childhood scenes. But this story opens my depiction of diaspora experiences, capturing the lives of Zimbabweans in the United States. Since I completed the first draft, ideas of similar stories have been flooding in. The process has so far been liberating. In writing the story, I followed the most informal, monologic style I have ever used, to allow Fati to tell his story with all its contadictions. In a way, the style allows for discovery as the story develops. I have been free to write in a way that enables a more organic depiction of character.

Running in Zimbabwe

JONATHAN BRAKARSH

1

It was another beautiful day in Harare. Ada Schmidt was going for a run. She jogged from her door down the driveway and made a right onto the street. Maybe it was the pull of magnetic north but she always went this way.

Ada Schmidt was German, with a slender, athletic body that was used to running several times a week. She had a face that was perfect for a soap commercial: radiant, slightly rose-tinted skin, with even, white teeth and a smile that could persuade you to buy anything.

As a single mother with two children and a demanding job, she ran in order to stay sane. When she saw the men coming toward her, she stopped. Like a movie preview, various scenes ran through her head:

- *Ada Schmidt is dragged into the bushes by a horde of hungry-eyed men.*
- *Ada Schmidt is surrounded by a mob, then marched to Harare Central Police Station for questioning.*

The line of men continued to move toward her, like a battering ram, their voices rising in unison, singing three-part harmony in rhythm with their pace. Feet clapping on the pavement, whistles piercing the air.

She imagined her Missing Persons poster. It would have her picture and read: 'German female, 32 years of age, out for a morning run with black spandex pants and a white T-shirt sporting the slogan, "Live/Love/Laugh".'

She stood paralysed as the men split into two columns around her. Some wore sweatshirts in olive green with white lettering stating 'ARMY'. Most of the men gave her a quick glance – some smiled, some greeted her, and some remained silent. 'Good morning,' she said. 'Good morning,' they replied, smiling as they passed.

II

His face no one ever seemed to remember, except for the tic that starred in its own conga line dance above his left eyebrow. The muscle below the skin would pulsate up and down and occasionally give a kick. He wore a white shirt, with only the collar button undone despite the warm weather, and dress pants with black shoes polished to a high shine. He possessed the body of a wrestler and twice had been high school state champion. Over time, most of his body turned to fat but his shoulders and arms remained as rolled bands of muscle. With his broad frame and height of almost two metres, he had worked as a loan collector and, briefly, as a movie actor in Asia. Now he starred in another occupation – flying across oceans, and then waiting. Waiting for a phone call. Waiting for a seemingly casual meal in a hotel restaurant with someone he would meet only once. His business card stated that he worked for a shipping company. He travelled a lot: Russia, China, Pakistan, and Nigeria. When people asked him what he did he said he was a 'Righter'. He considered this his purpose in life – to assist good causes.

At reception, he gave an address where he had never lived and a name that his mother would never know – Michael Stone. With its carpeted hallways, and heavy wooden doors, the Meikles Hotel provided a reassuring feeling of security. After unpacking, he went down to 'The Lounge', a spacious nook in the centre of the hotel lobby, where they served light snacks. Sitting down at a table with a view of the reception area, he took out his pad and began to write. He had written two detective novels that had achieved minor success and his publisher was asking for his third effort. This book was entitled *Too Many Ways to Kill*. He wanted a sandwich. A waiter was at the far end of the room. He raised his hand and waved. It was a busy lunch hour. Hoping to attract someone's attention, he snapped his fingers and looked around the room. He received some sympathetic smiles but nothing more.

Then from behind his right shoulder, he heard, 'Can I help you sir?'

Michael Stone startled, his body torquing in the direction of the voice, his arms reflexively coming up into fighting position. He smiled at the young, thin man in front of him who wore a white shirt, black vest and black bow tie.

'Yes,' he said, 'I would like a cheese sandwich, toasted, a small salad, and some tea.' The waiter nodded. 'What dressing would you like, sir?' 'Russian will do,' Stone replied.

'Yes sir,' the waiter said and moved away. Michael Stone returned to his writing, thinking about how the international diamond dealer had just died in the shower after using the bath soap that the Russian maid had stealthily injected with poison the night before. The poison? Quick acting and rapidly metabolised in the body, leaving no trace.

III

His arms and legs were aching. He wanted a massage badly. Running from the police was not his sport. It was supposed to have been an evening of academic discussion – Egypt, Tunisia – and what this might foretell for the future of Zimbabwe. He was an academic, black, smooth-faced, stomach falling over his belt, a bit overstuffed with too many conference lunches, hair short with sprouts of gray, and Armani glasses, a gift from his daughter, that matched his suit. Why he had worn a suit to the gathering he still couldn't figure out. Did he want to look like a Minister? Who did he want to impress? He had hoped that some donor organisations would be there, and that perhaps this year he could work with more than a subsistence budget.

Luckily, Professor Bernard Pochaya was in the toilet when it all happened. The police had charged into the church hall where an audience

3

of a hundred sat watching videos of the events in Egypt. 'Forty-six People Arrested!' the newspapers reported. He had spoken to his colleagues on the phone for hours last night about who had escaped. They were all confused, unsure of who was hiding and who had been imprisoned.

This morning he took a hot shower, but midway through the water became a dribble, then a slow drip, and then ceased to flow entirely. He dried himself, put on his bathrobe, a reminder of his stay at a swank hotel in Nairobi, and walked out of the door and up to the green plastic water tank perched on the hill behind his house. It was empty. He opened up the taps in his house – not a drop trickled out. He called his neighbour on the phone and was informed that this water stoppage was going to be a bad one – a pipe had burst a kilometre away. Under these circumstances he would visit the boreholes of his many friends, but these days either their boreholes were running dry, mixing generous amounts of mud with the water, or the constant power surges had blown their pumps, so there was no water to be had.

He ate breakfast, changed into respectable clothing, and went to the storage room, removing three plastic 20-litre water barrels, and putting them in the back of his truck. As he drove out of his gate, women were already heading in the direction of the burst water pipe, various shaped *chigubus* balanced on their heads, or tied to their bicycle handles or loaded into the back of their cars. It was like a village scene. Narrowly missing a pothole, he heard a sound like a drum being struck, but did not think much of it and kept driving. In his rear-view mirror he saw a car suddenly swerve as three green water barrels bounced into the centre of the road. He pulled over and climbed out of his vehicle.

The tailgate of his truck had opened and all the containers had rolled out. He swore under his breath and ran back to the truck, jumping into the driver's seat, jerking the ignition on sharply and making a U-turn. He scanned the street and high grass bordering the sidewalks for his containers.

He looked for groups of people fighting over his water barrels, which they probably thought had fallen from the sky like manna from heaven. There were no clues. He was cursing now. Where was everyone who'd

4

run off with his water containers? He passed two apostolic men, tall, thin, and bearded in white robes waiting patiently by the side of the road, holding a green water container. As soon as he approached them, they knew his purpose. They handed him the container with a smile. He thanked them. He returned to his truck and continued driving along the street, scanning the area intently. His *chigubus* had disappeared.

He followed the lines of people walking, like ants on a pheromone trail, to the source of the water. When he arrived, there was a big crowd of people patiently waiting their turn. Three people at a time dipped their pots into the large brown puddle being fed by a slow outpouring of water from the broken pipe. He pulled his one water barrel out of the truck and joined the others. He felt angry and humiliated. Here he was, a full professor, head of his department, winner of international awards and he was waiting in this long line like an earthquake victim, holding a dented, green plastic container.

Around him he heard lively conversation, familiar political jokes like the one about the man who was tired of waiting in an endless queue for petrol and decided to go to State House to complain, as he no longer cared about the consequences of his actions. He told his friend to keep his place in line, expecting to be back in several hours. Twenty minutes later he returned.

'What happened?' his friend asked. 'Why are you back so soon?' The man replied, 'The line outside State House was even longer than the line here.'

Uproarious laughter and clapping followed. Professor Pochaya remained in the queue fuming, thinking about leaving the country, dreaming of a lovely job at an American university with a big salary, big libraries, and respect. Every so often a friend or neighbour would drop by to interrupt his reverie.

'Ah,' they said, 'Long time!' or 'Great place to meet!' or 'We're going out for a drink after this, want to come?'

Bit by bit he began to relax, and sometimes smiled, surrounded by his friends and neighbours waving and joking. Circles of laughter rose like smoke rings into the sky.

IV

The host was a rich businessman who was making his money in life in-surance and wildlife conservation. The guests sipped drinks in the open-air lounge tiled with glitter stone, looking out over a fifty-acre plot where warthog and impala gambolled freely. There were Chinese lights strung across the width of the patio and down the stairs to the braai area. Professor Bernard Pochaya was having a drink with Ada Schmidt.

'We drive faster in Germany,' she said, 'but here in Zimbabwe peo-ple are always trying to cut in front of each other. It's like your cur-rency is soon going to become worthless again and everyone wants to be first in line at the bank to exchange it for new currency.' Professor Bernard Pochaya smiled, looking at her face and then at her shoes – black, slender, and stylish. While growing up, Bernard used to spend hours arranging shoes on shelves and hanging up dresses in his father's shop. He had a salesman's appreciation of a well-made shoe.

The music segued from hip-hop to Latin, music ripe for salsa. He felt a flush of heat to his face as if a silent hand was controlling his mouth, opening and closing his jaw like a ventriloquist's dummy. 'Would you like to dance?' he asked.

Ada looked at this rather overweight man with an earnest expression on his face. 'Yes,' she replied. 'I would be happy to dance.' They moved onto the dance floor, swaying hips and swinging arms. Though their bodies were wildly different, they danced with a unified grace. Time began running backwards as Bernard Pochaya watched Ada transform into his wife, long gone – sinuous, sexy, smiling, feet moving on the dance floor like a butterfly.

V

Many people had received e-mails announcing a protest in the park. Some people suspected that it was a ruling party plot to see who would turn up, and then arrest them. But the e-mail sounded real enough:

6

'Please come to a peaceful protest. Let them know! Tuesday, March 1st, 2011.'

Professor Bernard Pochaya was walking through the centre of town when he heard singing. Hundreds of people were walking along, holding up signs which read,

'We have something to say!'

'Enough!'

Professor Pochaya felt a flutter of excitement. Maybe this was it. This was the one, the spark that would finally bring change. Lines of police in riot gear were standing along the side of the street or in light grey trucks sitting and watching. Then, as if a dog whistle had been blown, the police came running – jumping out of their trucks, batons cutting through the air, Plexiglas face-guards down, some with shields and some just running with full force into the crowd swinging their batons in all directions. One policeman ran up the street grabbing at passers-by, knocking them down to the ground. He was moving in Professor Bernard Pochaya's direction.

Hearing the sound of steps behind him, the Professor began running. He was not fast enough. A policeman lunged at him, trapping his neck in the crook of his arm. Pochaya uttered a rapid prayer. To his surprise it was immediately answered. The policeman's grip loosened.

'*Sekuru!*' the man said, through his Plexiglas visor. 'What are you doing here?' It was his nephew, Tafadzwa, the second son of his father's middle brother. 'Sekuru, I'm going to have to punch you. My supervisor is watching. Just fall to the ground and stay there.'

Tafadzwa swung his baton into the Professor's solar plexus and Bernard saw the world shimmer in front of his eyes as all the breath left him. Then Tafadzwa gently pushed his uncle down to the ground. 'Just breathe slowly,' Tafadzwa said, 'you'll feel better in a minute.' The Professor tasted the pavement in his mouth. This entire exchange took thirty seconds. Already Tafadzwa was running up the block, warring, a gladiator ready to vanquish the non-believers. Professor Bernard Pochaya heard screams in the distance. After a few minutes he dared to raise his head. The world was blurry and he realised his glasses were

7

not on the bridge of his nose. He stood up and looked around him – they had bounced next to a cardboard box of rubbish. He picked them up, dusted them off, breathed on the lenses, wiping them on a clean section of his shirt – nothing was scratched. He felt relieved.

VI

Michael Stone waited for the bill. He was late for a meeting. His waiter had disappeared fifteen minutes previously. Mr Stone suspected that the waiter's shift had ended and he had gone home. He heard a noise and felt a sudden drop in air pressure. He looked out of the front doors of the hotel and saw the police running into the crowd, swinging their batons as if they were scythes harvesting wheat. He shook his head. 'What a fucked up country this is,' he thought. 'No one can do anything right.'

Ada Schmidt had gone to the old side of town to ZimSpice to pick up some paprika and ground cumin. She was thirsty and tired and wanted to stop for a cappuccino and a glass of water, but she was caught in traffic. Emergency taxis, filled with people, were trying to cut in front of her. She was driving a dominating Toyota Hilux twin cab that rode high and had plenty of power with a 3.2 litre engine. She was pleased when she intimidated an encroaching emergency taxi, pushing it to the side. In front of her, there was a polite war in progress – one car was trying to complete a U-turn, while five taxis and a truck were busy trying to go around it. Then a conductor got out of one of the emergency taxis and started directing traffic, motioning for Ada Schmidt to cut across one lane and turn left. She waved her thanks. She had wanted to go straight but that road was a solid block of cars that would not move any time soon. The 2 p.m. skies were darkening and she had to be at the International School in ten minutes to pick up her children. She was running late. There was no time to stop for coffee.

The rains came, washing away the police and the protesters. The water problem was solved for today as people lined up their buckets in the streets and children came out of their houses, laughing, sticking out their tongues, mouths upraised to the sky. Traffic slowed to a crawl.

Ada Schmidt was worried. Her children would be waiting and they would not know where she was.

Professor Bernard Pochaya looked up into the sky and felt the rain on his forehead. He looked down and saw the dirt tracks on his pants, the rain extending the stains downward. Knees hurting, he started to walk in the direction of his parked car. 'Live to fight another day,' he chuckled to himself.

VII

He had confidence that this meeting would make him a very rich man. Michael Stone drove his rented car towards the suburb of Mount Pleasant, watching the rain make patterns on his window, smelling the petrol fumes leaking into the passenger compartment. He wondered how long it would be before he could return home. A map was balanced on his left knee and he looked at the streets in frustration, as most had no signs.

Ada Schmidt was happy. Traffic had begun moving again. Suddenly, she felt a jolting impact and watched in slow motion as her door began to buckle and her car spun 90 degrees. Her head hit the windscreen hard. There was a bump in the centre of her forehead that was rapidly swelling and turning crimson. She felt dazed, but she was also angry. Ada Schmidt staggered onto the street.

A crowd had gathered around Michael Stone's car of with a mixture of fascination and concern. The bonnet was pushed in like an accordion. Michael Stone shoved open the door and stepped out onto the street, hastily stuffing a brown drawstring bag as big as a fist under his shirt and into the waistband of his pants. But the top of the bag was loose and two beautiful polished gems, facets catching the sun, fell to the street, bounced several times and lay still. There was a cheer of surprise from the crowd. He picked up the two diamonds and held them in his palm, as he watched two policemen push their way through the crowd. The policemen arrived and stood in front of him, momentarily assessing the situation.

'Let me smell your breath!' said one policeman. 'Let me see what is in your hand!' said the other policeman. The crowd began to chant 'Diamonds! Diamonds!' and they pushed closer to see how the drama would proceed.

Michael Stone held up one diamond and threw it into the crowd. The crowd went wild, diving and pushing to acquire the glittery prize. He then gave one diamond to the two policemen. 'Split it,' he said. The two policemen held the clear lustrous stone between them, fingers overlapping. Michael Stone climbed quickly into his car.

Meanwhile, Ada Schmidt, cursing loudly, was running through her voluminous list of German curses. She began walking, drunk with shock, moving crookedly in the direction of Michael Stone's car yelling 'You idiot, you almost killed me!' Observing him getting into his car, she became even more infuriated. She quickened her pace to a stumbling run, stepped into a pothole, and went sprawling onto the pavement. Michael Stone pressed his foot gently on the accelerator and drove off.

A half-block away, Bernard Pochaya had his attention diverted from his thoughts by the thump of the two cars colliding. Like a silent movie, he saw Ada Schmidt walking unsteadily out of her car, gesticulating, running, falling and now sitting in pain on the edge of a pothole, holding her ankle. Professor Bernard Pochaya hurried toward her, noticing that the strap of one of her shoes had broken. He reached the pothole where she crouched and picked her up, feeling the muscles of his lower back beginning to protest. Ada Schmidt balanced on one foot, leaning her weight against him, her arm around his neck as they walked. 'I think it's time to stop running,' he said. Ada Schmidt and Bernard Pochaya felt the soft surge of warmth between them and laughed.

Miss McConkey of Bridgewater Close

PETINA GAPPAH

When I saw her yesterday, Miss McConkey looked vital and frail at the same time, like a cross between Doris Lessing and poor murdered Cora Lansquenet in *After the Funeral*. She stood in the queue for the only cashier inside the OK supermarket that replaced the Bon Marché at Mabelreign shopping centre. She carried her head as she always had done, slightly tilted to the left, and her hair, all white now, was pinned into a large bun at the top of her head. When I was a little girl, her hair reminded me of Mam'zelle's at Mallory Towers. Not Mam'zelle Rougier, who was thin and sour and never any fun, but Mam'zelle Dupont who was plump and jolly. Her eyes, unlike Mam'zelle Dupont's, which were never still and sparkled and gleamed behind her lorgnettes, did not twinkle behind her round glasses. For all the time that had passed, I would have known her anywhere, and besides, you can count on all eight fingers the number of white people left in the whole of Mabel-reign, from Sentosa to Bluff Hill, from Meyrick Park to Cotswold Hills.

She took an inordinate amount of time to get her things onto the counter, sugar, and pasta, tomato puree, a packet of onions and two cans of condensed milk, Mazoe orange crush, a loaf of bread, a crate of eggs, seven packets of candles and three packets of Pedigree pet food.

'That will be seventy five billion three hundred million and six hundred thousand dollars,' the cashier said.

She took out four bricks of notes, unpeeled some from one and handed over the rest. The cashier took the bands off the bricks and put the money through a money counter.

When the whirring sound stopped, and the red button blinked to indicate the amount, the cashier said, 'It's short by five hundred million.'

'That can't be,' Miss McConkey said. 'Your machine must be broken. I have just this minute come from the bank.'

The cashier counted out the money, spreading the notes in little heaps of billions and millions across the counter. By now the line of shoppers holding their goods, mainly the packets of candles that had been rumoured to be available only at the OK in Mabelreign, were murmuring mutiny.

The counting continued.

The machine was not broken.

'Do you have enough?' asked the cashier.

'What?' said Miss McConkey.

The cashier scowled and sighed and said, 'Money. 'Do you have enough money?'

'More money,' Miss McConkey said.

'Pardon?' said the cashier.

'*More*, not *enough*. Have you more money?'

'Have you more money?' the cashier repeated loudly.

'There is no need to shout like that,' Miss McConkey said. 'Wait.'

She rummaged in her bag to find the notes she had unpeeled, but these with the others failed to add to seventy-five billion three hundred million and six hundred thousand dollars.

'Maybe you can go back to the bank and ask,' suggested the cashier.

'It's closed now, isn't it,' said Miss McConkey, 'and what's the use?'

'We can take some off,' the cashier said.

She reached for the pet food.

'I'll decide, thank you,' Miss McConkey said.

'*Kanotofidha zvako imbwa mari kasina,*' said a voice behind me.

I moved forward to the till.

'I know her,' I said to the cashier in Shona, and in English, to Miss McConkey, I said, 'I would be very happy to help you pay for your groceries.'

'No, thank you,' Miss McConkey said without looking at me.

'Miss McConkey,' I said.

She looked at me then.

'You live in Bridgewater Close,' I said. 'At number seventeen. I know your house, and I can always get the money from you later.'

I ignored the mutters coming from behind me and continued, 'You were my headmistress at HMS Junior.' Then I told her my name. She looked blank, and no wonder, I had given her my real name. I told her my school name.

'Of course', she said. 'You were in Kudu.'

'You've a good memory,' I said.

I gave her the money for her groceries, paid for mine, and after a tussle, she agreed that I could carry her bags to her car. Her car was parked on the other side of Stortford Parade, facing the market and the church. It was the yellow Datsun 120Y I remembered, the car that made my heart beat as I saw it drive past.

'I was not headmistress for long after you got there, was I?'

She looked straight into me, and I was a child again, the old fear gripped my heart, and I thought that she must know that it was because of me that she no longer stood on the stage in the hall, flanked between the two merit boards as all of HMS Junior, from KG1 to Grade 7Blue with one voice said, 'Good Morning, Miss McConkey.'

ᥕᥣ

We were always the first at the things that mattered to my parents. So it was no surprise to anyone when my parents moved to Cotswold Hills, when I was seven, the year that the white people who ran our country opened up the areas that they had closed to the blacks.

My father worked for a bank in town. Our family was the first in the street to own a car, a yellow Citroen called *bambadatya* in the township because of its crouching frog shape. I was the first child I ever knew to fly in an aeroplane, to Victoria Falls, not to see the waterfall but my father, who worked there briefly for six months.

For years after that, my mother kept the tickets stuck prominently in the photo album, next to a picture of us standing by the Air Rhodesia aircraft. When visitors asked to see the photo album, and they asked what the tickets were, my mother, in voice that worked too hard to be casual said, 'Oh, these are just plane tickets from the time we went to Vic Falls.' She made sure to call it Vic Falls because that is what the captain had said when we landed, 'Welcome to Vic Falls,' he said, 'on this bright and sunny day,' and she never called it anything else after that.

Shortly after the plane ride, but long after he bought the car, we moved out of Specimen and into Glen Norah B, to one of the smart flats that were a street from the township, where we were not the first to have a car, but we were the first to have both a telephone and a television. My father was not content to live in the African townships, in Mbare and Highfield, Mabvuku and Glen Norah; nor for him the African suburbs of Westwood, just one road from Kambuzuma, or Marimba Park, ten steps removed from Mufakose. On Sundays after church, he took us for long drives along Salisbury Drive and pointed out Borrowdale, Cotswold Hills, Marlborough and Mount Pleasant, Highlands, Avondale, Bluff Hill, places whose very names evoked wonderful lives that were closed to us because the Prime Minister had decreed that not in a thousand years would black people ever rule Rhodesia.

We moved in the year of the internal settlement. The houses were quiet on undusty streets. There were trees, flowers and lawns everywhere. There were green hedges, and low gates with signs on which a silhouetted dog snarled at man with the words "Beware of the dog, *bassopo la inja*". Milkmen deposited bottles of milk with gold and silver tops outside, and no one stole them. In our living room with a fireplace and a maroon, fitted carpet, we watched television adverts for Solo, the margarine for families with an appetite for life, for Pro-Nutro, the balance of nature, and Sunlight for that fresh, sharp clean. That Christ-

14

mas, my parents had a party for all our relatives. My father danced my mother around and around while David Scobie sang Gypsy Girl. All the guests cried *enko enko enko* so that by the time I went to sleep that night, I knew all the words to the song and the *tanatana tanatana tanatana* of the chorus wove its way into my dreams.

In January I started at my new school. It was called Henry Morton Stanley Junior School but everyone called it HMS Junior. On the morning of my first day, I met Miss McConkey. 'I can't pronounce Zvamaida,' she said, as she wrote my name down. She looked at my mother with great displeasure, as though my mother had named me just to disoblige her. 'Has she no other name?'

As it happened I did, my second name, Hester, named for my father's dead sister, a name I hated. I was lucky, I suppose, Lucia in Grade 3Red did not have any name other than Chioniso, so her mother plucked Lucia out of the air of Miss McConkey's office. Lucia sometimes forgot her new name and got into trouble with her teacher.

And so I left Zvamaida behind in Glen Norah, and Hester took her place, a Hester who missed the old school, where the voices of children chanting in unison could be heard chanting the twelve times table, or 'Sleep baby mine, the jackals by the river are calling soft across the dim lagoon where tufted rows of mealies stand aquiver under a silver moon.'

In March, all the five black children who had started school on the same day were called to Miss McConkey's office. A missing book had been found in the bag of Danny in Grade 5Red who was Danidzirai at home. One of us had been found to be a thief and a liar, she told us. She gave a long talk about standards, and when we looked down at our feet, in the manner of respectful African children trained not to look adults in the eye, she talked about the importance of not being shifty.

Danny's theft came to define our relationship to each other. Until other black children joined the school much later, the five of us were linked by the hard fact of our colour, but separated by the greater gulfs of sex and age, and above all, by an urgent need to show that we were not all like him. We wanted white friends, they had all the nice things,

15

they had different things in their sandwiches, like marmite and polony and cheese. They went to South Africa on holidays, and brought back smarties. They knew all the Van jokes and what you got when you crossed a kangaroo with a ball of string, what was black and white and red all over, what the biscuit said after it got run over, why the one-handed man crossed the road. For Christmas, they didn't get clothes from the Edgars red hanger sale that they wore to school on Civvies day, they got annuals, like *Misty* and *Jacky*, and the *Beano* and *Whizzer* and *Chips*. They got Rubik's cubes, and yo-yos, and Monopoly and Ludo. They could hold their breaths for two widths underwater, and sometimes, like Evan Smith, for two lengths. They had their own hockey sticks, tennis rackets, and cricket bats, and did not use the old worn ones belonging to the school. Their mothers got their name tags from Barbours; they did not sew them on with uneven hands. And their fathers' radios did not say *nditaki nzvee kwaAmato wandiona*, or have the Jarzin Man's exhortations to shop at Jarzin *kune zvekudya zvine mitengo yakaderera*.

The only white children who befriended us, at least in that first lonely year, were the misfits and outcasts, the children whose company everyone else shunned. Danny took up with Keith Culverton whose family was large enough to be African, whose two dogs were said to have rabies, and who often came to school dressed in the big shorts of his older brother. After Ian Moffat's mother caused a scene at the school when her husband ran off to live with Miss Adamson, who taught Grade 5Red, Ian Moffat turned from the humiliation and became friends with Vusani. When Antonia de Souza dropped the relay baton and made Sable come last at the inter-house races, and no one would play with her because she ran like a spastic (and besides, said Stacey Collins, she was not really European, just Portuguese) she talked mainly to Lucia. Lucia made Eland come first in the same race but was only given the shared trophy long after we had forgotten that it was she who had led Eland to victory.

And I had Lara, Lara Van Tonder, the only Van in a class addicted to Van jokes, fat Lara whom everyone began to call Blubber after Mrs

Crowther taught us about whales. She was too fat to run or swim and when she walked fast her breath came quickly in little hisses. Lara liked me to brush her hair a hundred strokes in the school playground, and she made me count each one. 'If you brush it enough, at least three times a day' she said, 'it will become golden, like Pauline Fossil in *Ballet Shoes.*' I did not believe this really, and besides, I much preferred Petrova to Pauline and Posy, but I did it anyway, because Lara had a pool at home that she could not swim in, so she sat with her legs dangling in the pool, while I splashed and picked up coins from the bottom of the pool, and I was happy because we were just like Darrel and Mary-Lou in *Mallory Towers.*

∽∾

Miss McConkey lived two streets away from our house, in Bridgewater Close, and she often passed me in her Datsun 120Y. I made sure to straighten my shoulders when I saw her car, or when I walked past her house to take the short way home. One time, as I walked down Pat Palmer Owen Drive with no shoes, enjoying the hard heat of the road under my feet, I saw her car and jumped and hid in the ditch until she passed.

At school, I saw her every day at assembly, and in the corridors when she saw us walking in clusters she said, 'Single file, children.' Only in the third term, as Prize-giving Night approached, did I see her frequently.

∽∾

It was the school tradition, we were told, for HMS Junior to celebrate on that night the discovery of David Livingstone by HM Stanley. There was a poem that the school recited, a long and active poem in which there was a Livingstone and a Stanley, lots of concerned people in England wondering what had happened to Livingstone and lots of natives doing dances and naming all the places Livingstone had discovered.

The star was Keir Timmons, the captain of Roan. He was Stanley in an explorer hat and declaimed, in a voice loud with concern: 'Oh, where is Dr Livingstone, Dr David Livingstone, who went away to

Africa to tread the track unbeaten?' Then twenty children, who were supposed to be the people in England said: 'We haven't had a letter for so long, perhaps we'd better send Mr HM Stanley, just to see if he's been eaten.'

'And sing with me in chorus,' said Keir as Stanley, 'while the natives do a romp-o!' The five of us, the five black children, then did the romp-o. In loud voices, we chanted, 'Nyasa and Zambesi and Cabango and Kabompo, Chambese and Ujiji and Ilala and Dilolo, Shapanga and Katanga, not forgetting Bangweolo!' We danced and stomped and danced some more. Danny and Vusani beat their drums like their lives depended on it. Lucia and I added a little flourish by trying to ululate like we had seen our mothers do. 'Well done children,' Miss McConkey said. We were the finest natives that the school had ever seen, she said.

⋖⋗

We did not perform on Prize-giving Night. My uncle Gift changed everything. He had fought in the war for independence as Comrade White Destroyer, and had returned with little patience for what he called diehard renegade elements. He worked in the Department of Youth Affairs and Employment Creation. He told his boss about our poem and his boss called someone at *The Herald*, and Miss McConkey was in the news and then she was not the headmistress any more.

A Coloured man called Mr Marchand became the new headmaster. The teachers, said my parents, would not work under him so they would all go to South Africa. Uncle Gift said good riddance because there was no place for diehard renegade elements in the country, but my mother was worried about the white teachers leaving because she wanted me to have a good accent.

I was never called to Miss McConkey's office again because she had no office. She stayed on, teaching the remedial class for the slow learners, until there were no white teachers left at the school and only a sprinkling of white children. I became so afraid of Miss McConkey that I took to going the long way home, down Pat Palmer Owen Drive and into Cotswold Way, and thus managed to avoid Bridgewater Close for the rest of my life at HMS Junior. When I left to go to secondary school, she was still teaching the remedial class, never knowing that it was I who had changed her life forever. I did not see her again until yesterday, when she ran out of money in OK.

◈

I carried her bag of groceries for her and walked her to her car.

'Out there then, are you?' she said.

'I live in Australia now, Miss McConkey,' I said. 'In Melbourne.'

I thought she would say something more and waited, but she said nothing as she got into her car. She closed the door and said, 'You make sure you come and get your money.'

'Yes, Miss McConkey,' I said.

'You run along now,' she said.

'Goodbye, Miss McConkey,' I said.

She started her car without another word, and drove into Stortford Parade, past the Polyclinic and Maternity Centre that used to be the veterinary surgery, and past Wessex Drive. I watched her until her car turned left into Harare Drive, the old Salisbury Drive along which my father had driven us a lifetime ago, showing us all the places that were closed to us. I watched Miss McConkey until she disappeared from my view.

Crossroads

TENDAI HUCHU

They took the stabilisers off too early when they handed my brother his first bicycle. I remember it clearly, a small red BMX with matching red wheels. My father had bought it from Jaggers wholesalers in the no-streetlight, one-street town-centre of my birth. I marvelled at it when he took it from out of its the packaging on the morning of my brother's sixth birthday. I suddenly wished I was much older – alas I was second born and felt second best. My yellow tricycle with its steel frame, solid rubber wheels and safety flag now looked childish compared to this wonderful new contraption.

I counted the months until my birthday. The only problem was, I wasn't too sure when it was. I was too busy with important things like catching frogs in-between playing cowboys and indians, climbing trees or hard at *chikweshe*.

My father spent the morning teaching my brother to ride on the quiet road that led to our house. We lived in a bungalow that belonged to the mine where my father was foreman. It was a red-roofed white building that was at the end of Shashi View, a street of identical homes. The mine owned the town. Beyond the road was a bush path. I thought we were at the very edge of civilisation. It was my forest then and I still think it belongs to me, even though years later, I would return and find the trees had been torn down and replaced with houses built as far as the eye can see. Progress, I suppose, but no one had bothered to tell me.

I followed behind them on my tricycle. My father was on his Black Horse – an adult-sized bicycle that seemed gigantic to me. My father too was a colossus, I could walk between his legs if he opened them wide enough. My brother wobbled beside him though he had a stabiliser on either side of his new bike. I was desperately trying to keep up but I didn't stand a chance. Their big wheels chewed up more tar than my tiny ones. I expended energy, peddling furiously as they casually pulled away. It was no contest. The handicap was too great to overcome. Kudos to the inventor of the bicycle-chain. I stopped and watched them until they were as small as me.

Once they reached the top of the street they turned back, the sun glistening on their spokes, their shadows behind them. I followed as they rode past me and stopped in front of our house where my mother in her nurse's uniform was beaming proudly at the gate.

'He's doing all right. I think he should try without the extra wheels,' my father said.

'Give him time, it's only his first day.' Mother was always more realistic. I clung to the hem of her dress trying to attract her attention.

'Nonsense, these boys walked before they crawled.' My father was referring to the fact that as toddlers my brother and I had taken to duck-walking, holding onto pieces of furniture until we were able to stand on our own. We skipped the crawling bit.

'I'm not sure…' Mother said hesitantly, but father was already removing the stabilisers. What did women know about cycling anyway?

⊱❧

That was all such a long time ago. As I sit down and loosen my tie, looking out through the double-glazed window onto the street from my penthouse, I hear myself sighing. My wife enters the room and kisses me with her thin lips. Her flowing hair brushes ever so gently against me. She has brought me a glass of goji juice in a narrow beaker. My trembling hand accepts this offer and under her watchful eye I gulp down the repulsive liquid. She urges me to down drink the last few drops and leaves the room, satisfied that I'm doing my bit. I'm always doing my bit.

My Blackberry rings. It's the office again, Phil calling. He mumbles something, I grunt back. I go move to my laptop and check my e-mails.

'I thought you promised that you weren't going to be working this evening?' my wife says, re-entering the living room. Her chest rises and falls slowly.

'It's the guys from the office. They have something I need to see urgently.' I download an attachment and flick through it, instantly noticing a dozen errors.

'But you promised.'

'I know babe, but come and see this.' She doesn't move. When you marry a woman who is not half as educated as you are, this is the price you pay.

'You're always finding excuses. I'm beginning to think you're not as into this as I am.' She walks away in a huff and bangs the bedroom door. I should follow her but I don't. We've been through this routine many times. I know the problem is hers, not mine.

I go to the window and peer down into the street below. How times have changed. The boy who grew up in wide-open spaces is now locked away and confined in a box in this a concrete jungle. The trees have been replaced by lampposts, the duikers, which bounded across the yard, have become cyclists, the predators have morphed into cars, birdsong has been replaced by their honking; the boy too has become a man. An old woman with a trolley walks by slowly along the pavement. Several young people pass her without so much as a nod of acknowledgement. She moves stoically, seemingly impervious to the incivility of the times. I shudder at the thought of greying hair and wrinkled skin. I am still youngish and I intend to stay that way. If I want to make partner in the firm then I must get back to work.

The traffic below makes a soothing hum as I settle down with my laptop. From the bedroom I hear the sound of soft sobbing cleverly calibrated to be just loud enough to reach the lounge. How much longer must I play these emotional games? I have half a mind to ignore her but a husband must do his duty. I raise myself up and walk barefoot across the costly off-white carpet she chose for us in our first year together. A van Gogh in the hallway looks down on me reproachfully. Yet another of her purchases. I would have bought something nice by a local artist but she wanted an imitation, to me another demonstration of her limitations.

I knock on the door gently. Her sobbing increases exponentially. Imagine that! A man having to knock on his own bedroom door! I open it gently and stand a short distance from the bed. Its red satin sheets dominate the entire room. They represent a time when she was trying to turn the room into our own little love nest. There's a dressing table dominated by various expensive perfumes and cosmetics on which she has spent what shopping money I've given her. The wardrobe too is bursting at the seams with clothes she never seems to wear. I move in and sit next to her, throwing my left arm around her shoulder.

She buries her head in my chest and says, 'Don't touch me.'

My hand is limp and I do not know what to do. I haven't paid lobola for this one, so I don't own her.

'All right hun, I won't do any work today, okay? Stop crying now.'

'It's not about your bloody work. Why does everything have to be about your fucking job?' Because I'm the one who pays the rent and puts food on your table, I want to answer, but I bite my tongue. I can never picture my father having this sort of conversation. No sir, he was from an era when men were men.

'Then what is it about?' I ask, my hand stroking her back.

'I want you to be honest with me,' she says and sighs, wiping the tears off her face. 'Do you really want to make this work?'

'Of course. How can you even doubt that?'

'I just don't think you're making an effort, or maybe mummy has found you a nice girl from the village.' There's nothing but spite in her voice.

'Oh come on. Here we go again.'

It's true that mother never particularly liked this one and wanted me to get marry someone nearer to home, but that was a long time ago. I fail to understand why my wife can't move on. I chose her, after all. On the wall a clock ticks. I like the sound of clocks, especially in the morning. It's a reassuring sound. I kiss her cheek and tell her that I'm not going anywhere. To cheer her up, I even offer to cook.

Tonight we'll have something healthy: vegetable risotto. What I'd really like is some sadza with *mufushwa* and a helping of *maguru* but these days we've become vegans. We no longer drink and she has given up smoking. We're up first thing in the morning to exercise. Of course, she has a whole list of the things we can and can't do. I believe that if we've been good, we may have a dollop of ice cream.

⋙⋘

After our meal, we decide to go for a walk, but not before we've stood side by side in the kitchen doing the dishes. I wash, she dries – we're big on teamwork these days. We go out into the road and find ourselves walking on a blanket of white snow and everything sparkles under the streetlights. I button up my coat and she puts her hand into my pocket. Our breath turns to mist and merges before rising high into a vapour of nothingness. We walk in silence leaving footprints behind us as we go. The neighbourhood is quiet now; this is a decent area to live. Maybe here in the open, beyond the confines of our flat, we can speak freely to one another.

'Have you given it some thought?' I ask, introducing a subject that has nearly pushed us over the edge.

She brushes some hair off her face and looks into the distance.

'You do know that I love you more than anything in the world and I want to be with you wherever you may be, but I don't think it's safe.' She continues, 'I watch the news when you're away at the firm and you should see some of the reports. It's just not the sort of place to raise a family.'

'They exaggerate; my parents live there,' I reply.

'The other thing is I don't want to be far away from my parents, either ...' She doesn't consider the fact that I want to be close to my parents as well – hers live just round the corner. Suddenly I realise that I'm living on borrowed time. My job, my possessions and even my wife are all things that will be returned to the natives when I pack my bags to leave. Still I'm a man and I must give her a chance to make the right decision. We reach the end of the street and stand at the crossroads. A bicycle is chained to the railings. My mind drifts ...

❧❧

I stood in my father's shadow clinging to mother's dress as we waited for my brother to ride out on his own. It was a bright morning and an owl with an ill-set biological clock hooted once. Opposite us were three girls, the neighbour's kids, our age, in dirty dresses, hanging on to their fence and intently watching the proceedings. Their big eyes blinked in unison. One of them had plaits with pink and white ribbons woven into them. I despised her then, not knowing that she was to be my first kiss a few years later. I managed to sneak them a disapproving glance but was quickly diverted to by the spectacle at hand.

Big brother took a deep breath. His left foot was placed on the ground and his right was on the pedal ready to take off at the signal. How I wished it were me. Maybe soon it would be my turn. I clawed my toes into the soft green grass. Our yard was on a slight incline and soon my brother would be travelling down the slope towards the chicken coop and the fence just behind. The coop was a homemade contraption of wood and wire mesh raised at least a metre off the ground, though this did nothing to deter the occasional python that snuck in and feasted to its heart content. Gorged, it would not be able to squeeze out of the coop and would lie in a corner digesting its meal. Whenever a python invaded like that, father would call the rangers from National Parks to take it away. Pythons are a protected species, so killing them was not an option. The Parks' men would bundle it into a sack and then dump it by the Mazowe River far far away.

The leaves of the giant *musawu* tree rustled in a light breeze. A few floated lazily to earth. The little green fruits were not yet ready but soon they would turn yellow and fall to the ground. Every day I made sure to check on their progress. Such trivial matters could not have been on my big brother's mind. I saw his knuckles tighten around the handles of his new bike. His eyes squinted a little and a thin vein ran along his temple, then he lurched off – father shouting encouraging words in his wake.

The girls at the fence over the road squealed in delight. I stepped out from under the shadow to see better. My brother shot off straight like an arrow. He leant forward and his shorts hugged his butt tightly. To me he was a dare-devil as he gained speed down the slope past the *musawu* tree. And then things began to go wrong. The bike developed a wobble, only slightly at first, exactly the sort of thing the stabilisers would have rectified. But with each correction he made, the wobbling grew worse. He steered to the right and then to the left, the front and the back of the bicycle no longer in perfect alignment.

'Use your brakes!' father shouted. Mother cried out after him and I provided the refrain. But my brother only gathered speed as he hurtled toward the chicken coop whose peaceful inhabitants were unaware of the danger coming their way. Our chorus of 'Brakes! Brakes!' seemed to reach big brother just in time. His right hand unclenched from the handlebar and he squeezed the brake. In a split second he went from sixty to nought. In that split second we should all have breathed a sigh of relief but if the front wheel was pulled to a sudden halt, the back wheel and the boy continued in a forward motion. As his new bike wheeled through the air, the boy rose higher and higher, somersaulting as he went. The girls by the fence squealed and clapped. Father cupped his hand over his mouth. Mother screamed, and big brother flew over the chicken coop and disappeared.

Mother was the first to run down the road. We arrived a few seconds later and found the small boy lying on his back with his eyes closed. Mother, forgetting all her nursing skills, buried her head in her hands and wailed. Father resorted to shouting big brother's name as if that alone would wake the dead. Maybe it did, for my brother coughed, opened his eyes and stood up. A little unsteady on his feet, he walked past mother, round the chicken coop and over to his bike, which he picked up and checked over like an old pro. Satisfied nothing was broken, he began to push it up the slope for another go.

✦✦

'…so that's my decision and I hope it's one you will respect,' she concludes.

I choose not to reply. There's so much more I can tell her, but where to begin? Words can only say so much. How can anyone describe the way the sun shines and its heat melts your limbs. It's impossible to teach her about the joys of wading through loud markets, surrounded by voices and laughter on all sides. Could I ever really hope to convince her of the beauty of living in wide-open spaces and breathing unpolluted air. What does she know about the joy of living in a place where everyone knows your name. Waking up to birdsong in the morning and watching the sunset over the savannah with a glass of Mukuyu.

We look into each other's eyes. Hers are as blue and clear as the sky over my home. And so the competition is now between her eyes and my sky. I look into her face and see nothing but warmth and beauty. Her straight nose is a little red in the cold air. I want nothing more than to ride off with her into the sunset. If only I can make her see that her happiness is something only I can guarantee. Africa is in my heart and in my being. She only has to look back a few millenia and to see that it is in hers too. So here we stand on this one winter's night, at the crossroads of two insignificant streets in London. We're in the same place but our hearts are oceans apart. She smiles and I return her smile.

'Let's go home.' I say. We begin to walk hand in hand into the night.

Time's Footprints

ETHEL IRENE KABWATO

*'August is a thunder-wind
of seasons in conflict
and we await, harassed,
the stroke of the Spirit.'*
Musaemura B. Zimunya
(from the poem 'It's Blowing')

He knew he would find her sitting on the big, flat rock by the river. She was scribbling in her diary again and seemed oblivious to the sound of the birds and the gurgling water of the Pungwe. She kept on writing, her small frame shadowing him from the big black diary that had almost become a part of her, part of the landscape he called home. He knew she had worn the pink, layered skirt for him.

She looked up, saw him coming, and quickly climbed down from the rock and ran towards him, her arms outstretched, her pink skirt floating and swirling around her. She was barefoot but the long skirt gracefully covered her small feet.

'Steve…?' He remembered what she wanted from him – a bouquet of flowers from the forest. When she drew closer he hugged her, then

28

took her hand and guided her through the trees. They started picking wild blooms and he tickled her nose with the flowers and watched her dreamily breathe in their aroma before she flung her head back and laughed. He joined in, savouring every moment that he was with her, knowing she would record this moment in her diary and he in his heart.

'Hannah…' He had to tell her how he felt.

There was a loud crashing sound. Steve woke up. He was sweating. The alarm clock was on the floor, broken. He sank back into his pillow and wiped the sweat from his forehead with the back of his hand. He closed his eyes again. The image of the pink skirt filled his mind. He wondered why this dream kept recurring. The news of Hannah's death still haunted him.

Steve had received the news just before he went to bed. The message was from his father. It was the first sms from him in three years since his emigration to England.

> Stephen, Hannah passed away yesterday morning at Hauna
> District hospital. We have informed her relatives. Yours Baba.

He told himself that even when Hannah was alive he had often dreamt of her, but now…? Was she trying to tell him something? Was she freeing him from his conscience? Had she forgiven him for leaving her alone with the children that night when members of the People's Army came looking for him? He kept telling himself that Hannah had been an attractive woman and could have moved on without him, despite their three children, but a small voice insisted that she could not have done so because he had promised to come back for them once he'd settled down in the United Kingdom. It had been one month before the June presidential elections when a group of villagers had stormed his father's homestead in Honde Valley demanding to see him. They had found Hannah and the children instead and he'd heard all the insults that were hurled at her from his hiding place in the banana plantations as she tried to calm the villagers down. Hannah was a negotiator but that night she failed to placate them. They'd started beating her up. Every cry and every scream tortured him but he did not come out of his hiding place. It was his father's intervention that had saved the day. He told them to kill him and not to touch his daughter-in-law. He spoke in a loud, authoritative voice so that all those in nearby homesteads would hear him. His father instructed them to stop what they were doing to her and to shed his blood if that is what they wanted from her. The group complied but not before Steve heard a sharp, painful scream from Hannah. He had known that whatever had happened at that moment was not something that he wanted to hear from his father or from Hannah. He told himself that for as long as he lived he would not be able to live with this memory, but he had. He had never discussed that night with her. In the morning he had packed his bag and left the village.

For the first time in three years he started sobbing. He knew that it was time to return home. He owed Hannah and the children this visit. After all, he had chosen not to remember his promise. Steve had to leave the comfort of his London flat and take the first flight home.

The cab that he hired in Mutare only took him to Masere Business Centre, a few kilometres away from Samaringa village where Hannah would be buried, and access was by a footpath. The August winds roughly fanned his cheeks as he followed the dirt track that led him far into the misty hills of Honde Valley. Downhill, he came to a stream and he dusted his shoes and took a long cool drink. Despite the dust and the wind he walked on. Each time Steve hit a stone he cursed in English. When he got to Samaringa Business Centre his curses were drowned by the thick accents of the township revellers.

Suddenly, the wind became stronger, blurring his vision. The dusty spirals from the township grounds rose as everyone scuttled for shelter in the shops. Steve stood rooted to the spot. The whirlwind enclosed him, dust biting his eyes. Steve sighed. It was the wind that Hannah loved most about this place, he thought; she used to say that on a windy day the Mtarazi Falls brim with life as they cascade down the mountains. The wind carries its whispers with it.

Emotion increased Steve's pace as he walked through the banana plantations, which were near the village, a project his father had pioneered when he was working for Agritex. He kept reminding himself that if Hannah had not died he would not be here. The plantations brought memories of that night in June 2008 when Hannah had screamed and he had felt hopeless as he hid among the giant banana leaves, like a stranger intruding on someone's privacy. As his wife's scream echoed in the thick darkness he knew he should surrender to the mob, and he also knew that he would not do so.

As he drew nearer, he heard voices rise in sad song. The wind carried the words. His father's deep baritone seemed to shake with emotion. The singing was punctuated with the wailing of women. The cries drowned the sound of the waters of the Pungwe as it wound its way to the Indian Ocean. Hannah's death had brought him home.

A muddy path branched out of the banana plantations. Steve followed it until he could see the funeral procession. They were going to the cemetery near the Pungwe. Hannah had once told him that she wanted to be buried near the river where she could listen to the sounds of the water at night. He had called her his 'mermaid'. On the day he left the village he had gone to the flat rock and stood there until the village boys who worked for his father had arrived. They helped him to cross into Mozambique. When they were on the other side, he hurriedly scribbled a note to his wife and his father and told them that he would send for them as soon as he had settled down 'wherever the wind was taking him'.

Women from the Mothers' Union were pall-bearers. He was not sure which faction of the church Hannah belonged to after the Good Shepherd Church had split into two factions. When they were still communicating she had sent him an e-mail in which she updated him on the latest developments at home. She told him that there had been political interference in the church and as a result the local priest had lost control of the church and was now conducting services under the *muhacha* tree near Masere. The 'Muhacha Tree' faction was not allowed to wear the blue and white church uniform and neither were they allowed by members of the other faction to use the Mufudzi Wakanaka hymn books or regalia. Hannah had even asked him to guess which side she was on. He had not bothered to respond. He moved forward when he saw his father. Steve noticed that Hannah's coffin was a cheap one made by the local carpenter, Mr Gatsi at Hauna.

'She has carried her simplicity to the grave,' he thought. Drawing nearer, he was unnoticed as his father opened the coffin. She looked rested and at peace in her red dress, surely a tribute to her vivacity. Steve was glad that the villagers had not, as habit demanded, buried her in her church uniform. Knowing Hannah, he did not doubt that she had had a hand in the selection of the dress while on her deathbed. She had always fussed about colours and hated to see him in grey or black, and he felt suddenly very conscious of the black shirt that he was wearing. Her eyes were closed. She did not look bitter. She was just as he had known her, but now it was too late, he could not talk to her and tell her that he had been granted asylum and wanted to take her and the children away from the village and away from the painful memories that haunted him.

She was a fighter and he respected that. She had continued to fight long after he had left the country. He felt a coward, standing there, his children observing him as if he were a stranger. If only he had come out of the banana plantations to face his enemies. She had done it for him and had paid the ultimate price. This, he was to learn when his father narrated Hannah's ordeal to the mourners gathered by the graveside. He recounted the events of that night in June when some villagers had descended on their homestead. Steve heard for the first time how masked men took turns to rape Hannah while his father and mother watched. He had known then as he hid in the banana plantation what they were doing to her but he simply did not have the strength and the courage to give away his life for her. Somehow as he sank deeper among the banana leaves, he had told himself that she would survive, no matter how much they hurt her. From the moment he met her he had known that she was a survivor. Of course, Hannah had been there to patch up his life. She had stood by him. She had fought his battles for him. His friends often joked that she was the one who wrote all the speeches he presented at the party meetings. He had laughed then but he had not told them that she was his 'think tank'. All the ideas for the speeches came from a simple village woman who had no interest in moving to the city. Now he listened as his father told people how she had survived this abuse as if nothing had happened to her but in the end had succumbed to cervical cancer.

They lowered Hannah's coffin into the grave while the women from the Mothers' Union sang. The rustling of the leaves and the sound of the river complemented their voices. Steve took photographs of the women, men and children who had gathered there. When they covered her coffin with gravel only dust rose from the ground and they watched as the men took turns to use the shovel. There were no flowers for Hannah, not even the mock plastic wreaths that were sold at Hauna Growth Point. No one had remembered, not even his brothers, that she loved the wild blooms from the Mtarazi forest. The men put a blue enamel dish on the grave. A broom made of the *zumbani* shrub was used to sweep the grave when all rites had been completed. The broom was put on the grave near the enamel dish. Close family members were the last ones to leave for the village. As Steve followed the procession home he told himself that he would take the children to Mutare and buy flowers for Hannah.

Later, Steve sneaked out of the house and made his way to the river. On arrival there he sat on the flat rock near Hannah's grave. In the stillness of the evening he thought he heard Hannah's singsong voice. He waited for her to approach but she did not. A sudden chilly wind blew from the river. He shook with the impact and groped his way in the thick darkness. The pale luminous moon shone above him and the wind brought with it whispers. He stopped to listen.

'Steve?' It was Hannah. He was back in the banana plantations and she was screaming.

'Hannah!' he shouted.

⊰⊱

Someone laughed. He then remembered that he had to look for her. A violent wind blew from the east. It lifted the enamel dish from the grave. He jumped back in fright. He felt the cold wind blowing on his face. He tried to cover it with his jacket but the wind roughly dragged it from him and left him clutching his ears. He shivered. Then the wailing began. It made him seem hopeless. His legs would not move. They wobbled like jelly. He opened his mouth but words would not come. He blinked and the dust in his mouth choked him. When he opened his eyes he saw the road, now black, moving towards him, edging its way through the mountain, swallowing up the river and the trees. It grew narrower as it twisted and curved on dangerous slopes. The rain made the road wet and slippery. He remembered Hannah's tortured voice. It was the same voice that was driven by the gusts of wind and the falling rain. It echoed over the hills and mountains.

They found him sprawled over his wife's grave the following morning when they went for *mumvumo*. He was clutching the remnants of the *zumbani* shrub in his right hand. Its green leaves covered his face. The blue enamel dish lay at his feet. It was Steve's daughter, Vimbai, who recognised her father's brown suede jacket.

'Daddy!' she shouted and moved forward. Sekuru, her great grandfather held her back. She shook her head and made another attempt to break free. Sekuru's grip became firmer.

Everyone seemed paralysed with shock and fear except Sekuru, who handed over Vimbai to Steve's father. The older women who were supposed to perform their rites that morning gave way to Sekuru, VaGufu, the oldest man in the village. He was feared and respected. He claimed that he had fought alongside Chief Makoni in the first Chimurenga. No one doubted this. The elders watched in silence as he knelt on Hannah's grave and started clapping his hands. His words were inaudible to the rest of the people. It was well before sunrise and the men who stood there trembled with fear. Steve's father was in a daze. He wondered if his son was still alive. Steve was afraid of death. As a child he would avoid passing through the cemetery of the pioneer missionaries at St John's Church on his way to school. He also remembered years back when he had been found lying in the bush. He had all his money and clothes on him but the chain of his favourite bicycle, 'Rajah', had been broken. For hours on end he had cycled on the footpath leading to his homestead. He could see the thatched huts from a distance but he could not get there. He pushed the pedals hard and the bicycle seemed to move but he remained in the same spot. He had told his wife and children what happened but they had all dismissed it as one of his tales after a drinking spree at Masere. He wondered if Steve had met a similar fate.

In a way, he wished it had been his son lying in that mound of earth by the river. Steve had brought him nothing but bitterness. He wanted to spit at him as he lay on top of Hannah's grave in his suede jacket and brown leather shoes but it would be Hannah he would be spitting on and she did not deserve such insults. He knew of people who had children who had gone to England and who now basked in the glory of their success. Steve had not sent money home. He had not even bothered to build a modest home for his wife or his parents. Their neighbours said they read about him in the papers and how he had risen within the party ranks. They told him about the monthly vigils that he organised abroad. It was Hannah who made him stronger. 'The fool!' his father muttered under his breath.

VaGufu removed the *zumbani* leaves from Steve's ashen face. He gave them to Vimbai. When the men removed him from Hannah's grave, he was in a trance. The women took the shrubs from Vimbai and ululated as they swept Hannah's grave and then returned the shrubs and the blue enamel dish. VaGufu and Steve's father clapped their hands in unison as the women ululated. When all rites had been done, the young men took turns to carry Steve back to the homestead. When they reached the village Sekuru Gufu instructed all the men to take Steve to the *dare* where they would watch over him until he regained consciousness.

What would he do next...? Would Hannah's death remove the last shreds of courage from him, or would he find strength in her spirit and assume the burdens that she had borne for him?

The Situation

DONNA KIRSTEIN

Sometimes I wonder what happened. Why did my world turn upside-down? They said that a situation had developed. A situation. If you asked me what it was, I might not answer. If you were asked what it was, or if you were asked what the truth was, the truth that waits behind any one place, behind any one set of events or any one person, what would you say? Without a doubt, there is little chance of your answer being correct and true for everyone. Maybe reading between the lines, maybe looking at the different stories (all of which are true by the way) might suggest a larger truth. Maybe it wouldn't. Maybe reading between the lines, maybe looking at pieces of all the different newspaper articles would only complicate everything.

Possibly all the interpretations, all the stories are wrong.

But perhaps they're all right. Is it possible for every version to be right? Only one thing is certain, the situation is what it is…

෴

In the beginning I was at school – I thought that the strikes just meant a day's holiday. A day without teachers and lessons. I didn't understand what inflation was. But now, I wonder at it all – I wonder at the ground and the sand between my toes. I find the red-mud-washed durawalls astounding. I try and work out what the situation is now, what the situation was then and my head hurts. I sometimes feel that the truth of it all is just around the corner. The truth is slippery and hidden in the shifting shadows that I can see out of the corner of my eyes. The closest I can come to an answer is that the truth of the situation is in the thesaurus. The word 'situation' can be replaced with 'state of affairs, circumstances, state, condition, location, position, site, place'; so perhaps the truth of it lies somewhere in the dirt, in the topsoil and the dust that coats the city.

Then again I might have made a mistake, I might have got it all wrong. The situation might be none of those things, it all depends on where you're standing or whether you think that you are falling or flying.

White waters roaring so far below the drumming helicopter
against that burning blue sky so small beneath the sky
and the shadows behind me are moving closer...
Smell the flatness from their armpits or is it from
me why won't someone stop me
Well, it all started some years ago, when they told the baas that the
farm
was being taken over by a local businessman who had 'reclaimed'
what was his and
cars don't stop, they just drive by and laugh, hooting at me while I stand
clutching...
Ow *this railing is hot burning my palms maybe they will turn the same red*
as my arms which are blistering red from this sun. I'm so not used to this
don't
look down look up and over into that wall of mist dissolving into a sky that
is
so different from home, what would they say if they knew what I was going
to do...

Because the situation out here has been deteriorating,
without any end in sight, the local currency is now
worthless.
This country has endured rampant inflation, critical
food and fuel shortages. The government has blamed the
collapse on Western sanctions. Last Christmas the national rate of inflation surpassed one hundred thousand
per cent, the highest in the world. There is also a serious cholera epidemic ravaging the area and because
local services have been non-existent for some time, the
disease is spreading rapidly. But we cannot know quite
how rapidly because we have only recently been allowed
to report from the country. There is a risk of the eco-
nomic crisis spreading: neighbouring countries are on
the verge of rioting...

their manner was so boastful and smug. They didn't know
the land or how to farm it and so it now lies a wasteland.
'dangerous and stupid,' they would say you go away on a holiday to that unsafe place
not clever my boy but they just believe everything the news tells them...
the real truth is hidden from the world because much of the land bleeds now.
Locals called this place the smoke that thunders listen to it rumble concentrate on
not falling over the edge don't look down listen to the roar see the Falls.
They threatened to kill us, they beat us up, the boss's wife – what they
did to her
– the horror of it, I can't talk about it, they, us too, had to leave the
farm for
think about something else, those animals that's it list the animals that...
I saw so many ... there's a crocodile on the shining black rock below
the bridge, all the way down there, it's making me dizzy, they say
when you fall you die before you hit the ground I hope that's not true especially as
there's no ground only water swirling over those black rocks no
some time. When we went back there was less violence, the problem was

...because of the influx of immigrants and refugees flooding across the borders. The current situation can be traced back to the violent seizure of land that began in 2000. The president maintains the reclamations were necessary because after years of colonial rule, much of the country's best land was owned by a small number of white farmers. The forced seizure of private property led to sharp falls in agricultural production and precipitated the collapse of the country's economy; however, the government insists that a long-running drought is to blame for the poor harvests. People everywhere, particularly in the rural areas, are starving and many are forced to survive on meagre grain handouts. Hundreds of thousands have emigrated, driven out by the crisis. The government's urban slum demolition in 2005 was allegedly an effort to boost law and order and encourage development however it resulted in the wanton destruction of the

still there because we left again, we lost everything.
stop thinking about the negative OK, just do this, just breathe and
it will be fine take out my wallet and check what's in it the photos...
See, remember that time you kept smiling for mom even though you fell out
the tree
red blood was everywhere the pain was white hot burning
but then it was okay so breathe in... the burning tar on the
The police were called but these people, these squatters are random
people,
our very own 'rent-a-mob' who have been paid to squat on our farm
and so
bridge behind smells sticky and bitter look up and out into the mist the waterfalls
thundering plummeting into the gorge... Are my shoelaces tied yes keep
arms outstretched and okay breathe in, breathe out it
the police don't, can't and won't do anything. They aren't helpful.
Despite eviction orders they haven't kicked the squatters off our land,
they drink and smoke pot.
is okay breathe slowly feel the sun prickle, it will
They claim they haven't got the manpower to help us. But now things

townships housing opposition supporters. The razing
of these 'illegal structures' has left some 700,000
people without jobs and homes. One day a man can be
in waiting for hours in a supermarket queue for
bread beside someone and the next night that same
person could be out on a farm with a machete vowing
to kill children and torturing both white farmers
and their black workers.Despite this, the economy
has stabilised in the last few months, analysts at-
tribute this to the legalisation of foreign curren-
cies and the coalition government that has
temporarily united the opposition and the ruling
parties. The local hospitals are open and function-
ing again. But the crisis is far from resolved,
farms are still being occupied and there are still
many issues that remain. However, hope and optimism
is spreading throughout the region. For the first

burn away thoughts, empty everything with each breath of
might get better. Not all the squatters were bad. One of the other
farms
air... open blue wide sky taste the water's mist
shared the land, the squatters only wanted a chance to make a life for
themselves
and now the farm is looking for labourers.
be anywhere else feel the water mist on the
In this country land is still life, and people,
my husband
air breathe in, breathe out
might be able to
white waters roaring
get a job.
let go
Then
step out

40

time in several years, the supermarket shelves are
full although prices for commodities are still very
high. It is hard work but the situation seems to be
improving. The country has weathered the crisis,
the people seem to have survived and with their
strong work ethic the possibilities are endless;
the country, once the breadbasket of Africa, might
recover. The land might recover. The remnants of
past empires prove that it can be done. Tourists
are returning to the area, the tourism industry is
recovering. The country has some of the finest natural wonders in the world and is particularly
renowned for its white-water rafting, bungi-jumping
and safaris. The country is home to diverse
wildlife:

a recent tourist told
of how he
went
bungee-jumping.
Bungee-jumping

we can	off the bridge
into air	at Victoria
rebuild	Falls and
drop	on safari
our	saw countless birds,
upside	insects,
lives,	buffalo,
down, sky	quiet
family	antelope herds rushing
below	through fields,
will	elephants that never
forever	forget.
come	Crocodiles

41

falling from blue
home.
heart explodes skin
Perhaps
sharp cliffs blur smooth
finally
so still
the situation
cold sharp
is
sting sprays blue
looking
bounce
up.

waiting
on water-slicked
rocks
while hippos
splash and
trees are
silhouetted
against blood-red
skies. Exiles
are slowly
returning:
life is
coming
back.

The Novel Citizen

IGNATIUS MABASA

Very few people noticed him, or if they did, they simply didn't care. Beggars and vagrants are Harare's landscape. I saw him sitting against a large pillar that supported the verandah of a shop downtown. The floor was dusty and littered with rubbish. His skin was unusually dark as if it had been smoked by tyre fumes. He was shivering. It was an unforgivingly cold day and yet all he wore was a pair of tight, blue, dirty shorts. He hugged himself closely, perhaps too closely, so that even I felt the pain of his cold taut body.

I took off my jacket and the chilly weather hit me with its calloused knuckles. I asked myself if what I'd done was not one of those impulsive, irrational actions that will be later regretted. But I felt pity for him. I walked over and greeted the vagrant, but all he did was mumble a reply. He had three fresh open wounds on his hunched back that looked like violent maul marks. They must have been painful because they were weeping silently. He looked young – perhaps thirty-five. His hair was unkempt and there were three unlit matchsticks poked into it. He seemed oblivious to the goings-on around him.

'Are you not very cold?' Mine was a stupid question. It was very obvious that he was freezing. I was relieved when he didn't answer.

'You need something warm,' I continued, ignoring the owlish expressions of the Saturday morning shoppers who cast passing glances at me that seemed to say, 'You're an idiot to talk to such a person!' Generally, most people think vagrants are mad, violent and unpredictable.

'Here, take this jacket. It'll keep you warm,' I said, offering him my sheepskin-lined corduroy jacket. 'You can keep it.'

'I don't need one. I'm okay,' he replied in an unnaturally guttural voice.

I was surprised, not by his voice, but by his refusing a jacket when he was wearing so little and was clearly very cold.

'Look here *shamwari*, you need something warm. See how you're shivering. This cold is not good for you; you'll get pneumonia.'

For the first time he raised his head and looked at me. There was a strange fear and sadness in his eyes, which were like those of a butchered cow, its tongue foolishly protruding.

'Take the jacket. Please.' I was beginning to feel stupid with my hands outstretched, offering up a garment that blew forlornly in the cold air between us.

'No,' he said in a decisive voice that made me realise he would never accept the gift, no matter how well intentioned.

'Okay, *shamwari*, as you wish. But if I may ask, what are you doing out here in the open?'

'I should be asking you why I'm here. Do I deserve to be here?' His voice was spiced with anger. He was not looking at me but neither was he looking at anything in particular.

I didn't know what to say. I realised I'd asked without thinking and my question was insensitive. To save face, I said, 'You see, I think everybody must have a home, a family, friends, relatives. You cannot sit here forever in this cold weather. Where do you come from? Where are your people?'

'I'm a character from a novel.' His calm reply astonished me, making me wonder if all the quizzical looks I'd been receiving from passersby had been justified. This fellow must surely be nuts!

'A novel? What novel? What do you mean? Whose novel?' I swallowed as I tried to digest his dubious, seemingly ridiculous statement.

'I come from a novel by Judas Zino called The Dead are not Dead.'

I knew all Judas Zino's books, including his last one, which I had reviewed for a local newspaper, but the man was speaking of a title of which I'd never heard. I was not sure whether to continue with the conversation or conclude it before I was sucked into a treacherous vortex of vagrant mysteries. Yet, curiosity urged me to push the door to this man's heart and soul a little wider.

'I don't understand. Do you mean that there's a character based on your life in Zino's novel?'

'No. I've escaped from the pages of the book itself.'

I was fascinated by his strange revelation. I needed time to process his words, yet there was a small inner voice whispering, 'I'm warning you, leave this mad vagrant alone before you become entangled.' I paid no attention to it though I felt ambivalent.

'If you're a character from …' I hesitated a little. '…er this novel, as you say, then why are you here? How did you escape from the pages of the book into the real world?'

He looked at me witheringly as if to say, 'Do you call this the real world? You must be joking!' We eyed each other, then he asked, suddenly looking very serious, 'Do you really want to hear my story?'

I nodded. It was the best I could do because my mouth was not ready to say the word 'yes' and volunteer myself to hearing this stranger's story. Sometimes in life we commit ourselves to seemingly insignificant things such as listening to someone's life history, only to end up casseroled in the plot pot.

'Sit down!' His voice was a command

I sat down next to him on the dirty verandah. The floor was so cold that I could feel my bottom preparing to sneeze! I wondered what my wife would say if she found me talking to this filthy vagrant. I did not sit too close to him. His body had a pungent, fishy smell and besides, people stampeding down the pavement in front of us were looking at me quizzically. Human eyes can sometimes bite.

Then he spoke, sounding like somebody reading from an invisible but sacred book. 'Writers are merely brokers labelled geniuses and credited for meddling with our world. They pry into our lives and purport to create people, but when the characters become alive, like Frankenstein, they don't know what to do. Why? Because the characters want their freedom while the writer wants to control.' His sigh was very sad.

Then he continued, 'Most writers are weak. They can't stand being challenged by the characters they think they've created. They want control. There is no democracy in novels – we're victims of the pen-wielding writer because through the pen the writer has the power to determine what you say, even if it is not what you wanted to say.'

'You mean putting words in your mouth?' I wanted to assure him that I was listening.

'Yes, but it's even more heinous than that.' He looked at me with bayonet eyes. 'Through the pen, Judas wanted to determine what I thought, but I strongly resisted. Then, he felt threatened because he said I was free-spirited and larger than life and so he resorted to murder to eliminate me.'

He sniffed before resuming. 'There's blood on the hands of writers. They kill characters without even giving them a decent burial or allowing the other characters to ask questions or give them a period to mourn their colleagues. I think writers should leave creation matters to God because through their so-called creativity, they are controlling what we say and do – even how we dress and when we must sin. That makes novels unexciting for us, the citizens of the novel. Take my case, for example. Judas was always setting me up, expecting me to be grateful for being included in his fiction, yet I am the person who helped him tell our story because, as I told him, we, the characters, have a better understanding of the world, which he is struggling to portray, because we live there. We are citizens of the novel – even when Judas retires to bed, we the characters continue talking and living our lives. Life does not end in the writer's full stop. A writer is merely a conduit. This is why I arranged for the others not to speak or do anything, and what was the result? Poor Judas was stuck. He told his friends and his editor that he was suffering from writer's block. It was not a block, it was a strike by the citizens of the novel – some way of trying to make him listen to and respect us!'

I couldn't believe what I was hearing, and was trying to absorb the meaning of this strange man's words. I sighed, more to urge him on than anything else. I didn't want him to lose the plot even if I did not fully understand it. I was intrigued by his story and I tried to reconcile his persective on 'our' highly respected and multi-award winning Judas Zino. In a court of law, these would be very serious allegations indeed.

'Do I have to be a victim of Judas's violence? I have tried to teach Judas that using violence to solve a problem always results in worse problems. Do I have to be punished and banished for thinking and speaking ahead of him, for existing before he existed, for knowing the story he's trying to write before he began writing it? Do I have to be victimised for resurrecting all the colourful characters he killed?'

I didn't answer. I was not sure if I was supposed to answer this seemingly rhetorical question.

'You see, sir,' he continued, 'I've been flipping the pages of my life and I've disagreed with Judas about who I am and what he wants me to be. I told him that I have been very patient with him, allowing him to write my life, my character, put words in my mouth and think for me. I was giving him a chance, hoping that he was responsible and that he would know when to allow me to speak my mind and tell what I know. I've been reading the pages of the story he's writing – my story, my people's story – and I've realised that as long as we don't challenge him to let us to speak for ourselves, and marry who we want and when we want, there will be chaos, death, incest and melodrama: the story will simply play to the gallery.'

I nodded.

'I know that Judas's readers love drama, suspense, intrigue, but that has cost us dearly. Judas's publishers love tragedy, but that does not mean he should kill us ruthlessly so as to please his accomplices. Judas has been struggling to move on ever since he killed Skuza, a colourful character. I told him that Skuza was the soul of his story but he scoffed at me saying, "What has straw in common with wheat?" The paradox is that his editor has been phoning the poor chap ever since enquiring about his progress. Meantime, I've been watching him day after day – he sits down to write, stops, crosses out words and sentences, sighs, buries his head in his hands, and goes out to smoke. After some minutes, he returns smelling of fresh cigarettes. He writes, stops, gets up, makes coffee, drinks it, makes more coffee, smokes, sighs and returns to his notebook, scribbles, stops, stares into open space, buries his head in his hands, and tears the pages from his notebook, including the finished chapter. He confuses us. "Mere anarchy is loosed upon the world." Judas shreds pages, shreds words, strips away our world and the things we said and did yesterday, last week, last month, last year – leaving us gasping for air. What is the future without the past? Does the past not signpost the future?'

I felt out of my depth. So, I just sat like a mannequin, letting all the pins of fact and fiction prick me.

'Now sir, tell me, where is freedom when the writer wants to be the writer *and* the characters? Imagine a bus driver wanting to be a passenger in his own bus – what happens when he reaches his destination? Are there not passengers waiting to be driven on to destinations ahead? We, characters, don't try to be writers – yet writers want to have their cake and eat it! Why can't there be separation of powers? These sorts of problems create revolutions. We cannot have Judas write to please his publishing house and editor. He should respect our choices and dreams. Besides, what he refers to as 'his voice' is not his voice but our naked, raped and disgraced voice. He must be sincere and honourable and put an end to this big show of his. I suggested that he use death as a metaphor instead of killing off his characters, but he's headstrong, he told me I know nothing about writing. Dare Judas accuse me of knowing nothing about writing? I, Prose, the son of Allegory and his sweet wife Metaphor. Your award-winning writer tells me the obvious that when all is said and done the novel will bear his name; that he has it all planned and already knows how everything will end. He says he has discussed his idea with his editor and publisher and they both agree that his new novel will be very well received by the market. But if this

48

is so, why is Zino suffering from writer's block? Blank pages and silent characters are the script of nightmares.'

It seemed sighing had become my new language, so I sighed, having no other words for the vagrant.

'Sir, do you believe in predestination?'

Caught off guard, I was vague, 'I suppose it all depends with whom or where you are and what your persuasion is.'

Ignoring my response without even a sigh, he continued, 'You see, sir, predestination does not work in novels and has never worked in religion. The great book of God says our creator does not want us to perish; while some argue that God has already chosen those that he wants to go to either heaven or hell; but I know that a believer is also a creature of choice – capable of rejecting the Christ who died for him even if he knows the consequences of his act. Yet, God continues to be merciful – he does not use his ancient weapons of fire and brimstone to rein in sinners.

'Have you read Jacques Ellul's *Anarchy and Christianity?*' he asked, smiling for the first time. It was an interesting discovery, to notice his teeth: he had perfect, milky white teeth that did not quite match his general appearance.

'I'm sorry, I haven't read or heard of Jacques Ellul,' I said truthfully.

Then, the citizen of the novel said in an unassuming manner, 'You must get a copy. It is a book full of wisdom and revelation, but now I will tell you what Jacques Ellul said, which Judas should learn from. "No matter what God's power may be, the first aspect of God is never that of the absolute Master, the Almighty. It is that of the God who puts himself on our human level and limits himself."

'Judas must learn to limit himself, to give characters a choice whether to live or die. You now that even though God is referred to as a 'King', he has never acted in that capacity. He never takes control of his people's choices.'

He paused and swallowed hard before resuming. 'You see these scars on my back?'

I nodded, wanting him to talk rather than ask me questions.

'They're the result of Judas evicting me from our home, from the novel. He became angry with me, he said I was a stumbling-block – like a stubborn donkey standing in the middle of a road flapping its long ears and not heeding insults. Stupid Judas. Anyway, it doesn't matter anymore, I'm dying tonight: this is what Judas has planned. He says he's liberating me to write my own novel and tell my own story. And so here I am sitting with you, away from my world, from my people, from my life. I am not afraid of death, I died in the novel yesterday – and for your own information, death is the sweetest thing God invented. Death is sweeter than a layer of caramel over chocolate. Death frees you from politics, from thinking, from trying – when it's time to die, you die and you feel yourself disappearing into calmness, into mellowness and you become light and right. I am looking forward to my second and final death tonight; but I will not be killed by Judas. Before he looks for me, before he finds me, I will be dead. All he will discover is a beautiful smiling corpse. A happy corpse. This will be my way of striking back at Judas. It is my way of defeating him, then he will be forced to write about how he found me dead when he wanted to enjoy killing me.'

Then, with soft beseeching eyes he said, 'Sir, I'm not a writer, but as I've told you, I am dying tonight. Will you be kind enough to write this story just as I have told it to you? It will be the missing chapter in Judas's novel, it will be my voice, it will be my valedictory letter to my fellow citizens who may still be wondering what became of me after I disappeared from our world. But, more importantly, what you will write will be my epitaph. Will you do this for me?'

I sighed and said, 'I'm also not a writer and don't have the skills of Judas Zino, who has won numerous awards, but I will try to write your story. I hope I shall do it faithfully and allow your voice to come through truthfully.'

'You'll be fine. As Prose, the son of Allegory and his wife Metaphor, I'm ordaining you a writer now. You're writing my story and you do not have a publisher, so just go for it.' With those words, he stood up, yawned, stretched and limped off, joining the herd of Saturday morning shoppers and leaving me holding my jacket in my hands with his story in my heart, surrounded by litter on the verandah.

I stood up to go, but I couldn't move. I had been listening to this stranger for close to an hour. I had become oblivious of my body and everything around me. I looked in the direction that Prose, the citizen of the novel, had gone, but he was lost to human traffic. I shook my head and muttered, 'this story is stranger than fiction...'

An Intricate Deception

DANIEL MANDISHONA

The future is born from the seeds of the present, George, but it always carries with it the ashes of the past.

When you married Helen, you didn't tell her much about yourself. She didn't ask too many questions and you didn't volunteer unsolicited information. Let sleeping dogs lie – that has always been your policy. But little things about you had started bothering her. Your late nights, the white shirts smudged with lipstick she would silently show you before stuffing them into the washing machine. And those telephone calls that came at odd hours of the day. Soon, something would have to give. Every piece of string has its breaking point, George.

That wet and windy Thursday was the first time the two of you had exchanged blows. You were worried because this was an unacceptable escalation to your domestic squabbles. To make matters worse, Helen was eight months pregnant. The fighting could have induced a miscarriage or, worse still, caused harm to the unborn baby. But she was the one who had thrown the first punch. Your reaction had been instinctive – the natural defensive reflex of a cornered animal. You had been absent-minded that morning, having stayed up late watching the unrest sweeping through the Arab states. Late for work, you had forgotten your cell phone on the kitchen table. When you came back that evening, the damage had already been done. She told you she had gone through all your text messages – received and sent – and needed some answers.

'My cell phone is private. You had no right to do what you did.'

'It kept ringing so in the end I answered it. Some young girl called Martha.'

'I don't know anybody by that name.'

'She knows you. She called you Mr George. That's funny.'

'I never answer your phone when it rings in your absence.'

'I wondered where all your money was going to. Now I know. Sophie, Melissa, Debra, Julie, Ruth, Linda, Martha. It must be expensive to maintain all those ladies, Mr George...'

'You can't assume because I have female names in my phone book they are my girlfriends.'

'If they are your relatives how come I have never heard of them, never seen them and never heard you mention them?'

◈

You needed time to cool down, to realign your scrambled emotions. You had walked out of the flat, leaving her naked and sobbing in the bathroom. You needed time to think, to pull yourself together. It was well after midnight but your state of mind gave you the sort of Dutch courage that can make an angry man walk through fire. It was a moonlit night and there was a cool breeze. You decided against taking the car. The city centre was only a brisk ten-minute walk away. Martha was a wild teenager you had met the previous weekend at a city-centre club. She called you 'Mr George' because she was sixteen and you were forty-seven. You had bought her drinks, given her money for a pedicure and to get her hair done. Nothing serious had happened, mainly because she had to be home in Arcadia by midnight.

You walked past the American Embassy, a building so heavily barricaded it looked more like a medieval fortress than a diplomatic mission. Armed security guards patrolled the compound's peripheries. Pedestrians who walked past were viewed with a mixture of apprehension and suspicion. America might be the world's most powerful nation, you found yourself thinking, but it is also the world's most fearful. Your first stop was a popular sports club near the park. It was the end of the month but there weren't many people inside. A couple of elderly drunks sat by the bar, eyes glued on the television. The unfolding CNN news story said a Libyan diplomat in America had resigned his post in protest at the bloodshed on the streets of Tripoli.

'Gaddafi now has the blood of so many of his people on his hands,' said the former ambassador, 'and it will not be possible for the new country born after his departure to easily dislodge the baggage of this evil man's violent legacy.'

In Cairo, according to the CNN report, sympathetic protestors were massed in front of the Libyan embassy to register their displeasure. Libyan soldiers had also defected, declaring themselves champions of the people's cause. 'We shall free the country from the unholy grip of the tyrant Gaddafi,' declared a female protestor standing on top of an armoured vehicle. 'Of course there will be bloodshed, because freedom without sacrifice is like a mirage in the desert. All of us are prepared to die for our freedom.'

⋄⋄⋄

The beers in the sports club were warm and expensive. You switched to brandy and coke. The barman smiled apologetically, informed you there was no ice. You watched the American Secretary of State speaking on television about the political turmoil in North Africa.

'Leaders who deny their people democratic space should know that in the end they will just fuel the same instability they claim to fear.'

There was a real possibility of heartburn from the warm alcohol, so you left after less than fifteen minutes. You thought of Helen, alone in the flat and sobbing herself to sleep. You walked eastwards, towards the outer limits of the Central Business District. Your reflection dissolved in the puddles around your feet. A lone telephone rang in an empty office building behind a huge billboard, its dissonant echo swirling into the silence like a refrain from a forgotten lament. Thunder rolled in the distance. Drizzle started dripping from a ruptured sky. A tramp walking in front of you farted, laughed and then broke into an uneasy trot. A pair of street kids who had just emerged from a storm-water drain stood on the side of the pavement, limbering up to disengage their malnourished bodies from the inertia of sleep. Further up the road, more street kids crawled out of the drains like creatures emerging from long hibernations.

෴

Your first argument with Helen had been over money. You had come home late, after having shared a few drinks with some work colleagues. Martha, the wild teenager from Arcadia, had shared part of the evening with you. When you got home you found Helen had already retired to bed, her upper body propped up on a formidable mound of pillows.

'I made a list of the things I want to buy for the baby's nursery,' she had said excitedly. After she became pregnant you had moved to a more spacious two-bedroom flat. She had dedicated the small spare bedroom as the room where your first child would spend its first days on earth. She had painted the walls a bright pink and made curtains with an intricate lace trim. She kept the spare bedroom door locked and overnight visitors to the apartment had to spend the night on the ancient settee in the lounge.

'Nancy offered to give us stuff from her last baby.' Nancy was your elder sister, the proud mother of three noisy daughters.

'Nancy's children are all girls, George. The scan said ours is a boy.'

'It doesn't matter, Helen. Babies can wear anything.'

'My first-born is not going to wear hand-me-downs.

'Nancy is my sister...'

'It doesn't matter. I'm not giving birth to a second-hand baby, so why should he wear second-hand things?'

'That's not a nice thing to say.'

'Well, if you didn't spend so much money on alcohol and women I'm sure we could easily afford some of these small things.'

The war of words had escalated rapidly after that. Her anger has always been poised on the edge of a steep trajectory.

෴

You continued walking. Slightly out of breath, you reduced your pace. In the harsh street light your shadow followed you everywhere, like skin that cannot separate itself from flesh. Your tired feet weighed you down like lead. Every movement you made required your full concentration. Bob Dylan wailed from the radio of a passing car:

'The answer my friend, is blowing in the wind...'

A car packed with rowdy youngsters careered down a dual carriageway named after a dead African president, zigzagging past a red traffic light and splashing water on a bemused man standing alone in a bus stop. The sticker on the car's rear window briefly caught your attention. *Don't Steal: The Government Hates Competition.* A light mist clung to the glazed facades of high-rise buildings like moss.

Ten minutes later you walked past the city's largest referral hospital – a depressing structure of grey bricks, asbestos roofs and vast and endless corridors. In the old days it used to be for whites only. But after Independence ushered in the long-awaited era of freedom in 1980, the hospital had to treat all those who come to its doors regardless of race, colour, religion or creed. As a consequence standards plummeted dramatically. Those who can afford it now choose the private clinics and hospitals. You knew this place well because Uncle Gideon, your father's elder brother, spent his last pained days here.

You remember how the accident and casualty department looked like one of those makeshift field hospitals that always sprout up in the aftermath of catastrophic disasters. You remember how the admissions clerks chewed gum and took notes in laborious long hand. They were loud, rude and unsympathetic and always made it very clear they didn't like talking to people, especially sick ones. You remember how some of the sick littered the floor, waiting for attention. Those able to walk wandered around aimlessly, unsure what to do or where to go. For those lucky enough to be admitted into the wards, there was always a shortage of essential drugs, and electricity and running water were not always guaranteed. Relatives of the sick had to bring their own drips. In the entrance lobby, hung high above this man-made confusion, was a framed photograph of the country's first black doctor – the man the hospital was named after.

≪≫

Uncle Gideon's survival chances were between slim and zero. You could see it in the nurses' body language as they walked past. You could see it in the way the elderly cleaners gave you smiles of sympathy and prolonged greetings as they mopped the floor around your feet. Because you worked close by, you were always the first one to arrive at visiting time. You would loiter outside the main front entrance like a criminal compelled by guilt to return to the scene of a crime. Each evening, you jostled with the sweaty and restless crowds at the bottom of the narrow stairwell. You remember how, in the crowded wards, the harsh fluorescent lights illuminated the ghostly faces of the sick and the dying, and the drips by their bedsides bulged with strange liquids. You remember walking through the wheezing of those afflicted by chronic respiratory diseases and the final silent pains of those about to confront an inevitable destiny. You remember walking past the huddled conferences of families who had just received bad news, and you remember overhearing the whispered prayers of desperate relatives still hoping for last-minute miracles.

You always approached Uncle Gideon's bed in an indirect but measured stalk, like an animal avoiding the lair of a known predator. Uncle Gideon's bed, isolated at the end by the bay window, was always bathed in bluish grey sunlight. Always a meticulous and clean-shaven man, a straggly stipple of growth had now taken root on his hollowed out cheeks. You would walk towards the bed on tiptoe as if afraid the earth might explode beneath your feet. In the heat of the room the sweat would drip down the small of your back, stinging your skin like nettles. After a few visits you knew this man's illness was a slow process with a predetermined end – a biological inevitability. He was trapped between an unendurable life and an unreachable one. But the doctors always assured you they were doing their best.

'But sometimes even modern medicine has its limits,' one of them once told you. 'Whatever happens now is at the mercy of the gods.'

≪≫

Your father died when you were eight and Uncle Gideon brought you up as if you were one of his own. It was Uncle Gideon, a disillusioned nationalist who had spent ten years in detention, who gave you your first insight into the politics of Africa. You learnt from him how the newly independent states gave themselves African names but adopted western modes of government. You learnt how the western powers praised those whose regimes they propped up and how they dazzled with gifts of money and 'aid' those whose countries had resources that could become bridges to eternal prosperity. Praise will make a good man better, he told you, but it will often make a bad one worse. In most of the newly independent countries celebration soon turned to trepidation, joy was replaced by fear and the ululations of elation were soon replaced by sighs of misery. And according to Uncle Gideon, the tenet that has always guided Africa's autocratic rulers is that if you can divide, you can rule.

Uncle Gideon told you that 'free and fair' elections were always a smokescreen, because those already holding power had no intention of relinquishing it, just as a hungry dog does not easily give up its bone. You learnt how the ruling parties amended constitutions and rigged elections to ensure the opposition parties remained just that – opposition parties. You learnt that in Africa multiparty democracy was always going to be an alien paradigm, the pluralism of convenience. You learnt that when the promises made before Independence did not materialise, those with the power replaced disastrous populist policies with bogus and borrowed dogmas to counter the disillusionment and disaffection of their failed nationalism.

And you learnt from Uncle Gideon that peace did not always follow sacrifice; that it would always be a question of 'one man, one vote', once. You learnt that African rulers have always been patriarchal and autocratic; the biggest bull in the herd is always master – the one with the loudest voice speaks for all. But force, no matter how well concealed, always begets resistance. Uncle Gideon told you that the weak never win wars, George, because God is always on the side of the big battalions. And if you can hold people in fear for a single day, you can

58

hold them in fear for a hundred years. But the events in North Africa were proving how such a dangerous creed has its drawbacks; that it can be, and often is, a prelude to total madness. Terror is an effective means of control, George. History has shown that there is no dissent where there is order, that there is no chaos where there is compliance. But what our African leaders always forget is that man has responsibility, George, not power. Politics is, and will always be, a game of intricate deceptions.

❧

The skies above you have cleared. The heat that reached its peak at midday has dissipated completely, leaving behind a balmy haze. Above you, a sliver of moon slides in and out of the dark clouds like a sliced fingernail. A cat lies dead in the dirt by the side of the road, its head flattened by a passing vehicle, its stomach inflated like a balloon. It reminds you of the time when you were about nine and a dead dog lay outside the school gates for almost two weeks. With each passing day you witnessed the slow putrefaction of its flesh.

You are still trying to make plans for a future that has too many variables. Helen wants five children, you want two. She wants you to get another job, but you are happy where you are. When you seriously think about it, your entire existence has been one calamity after another. Helen was the one bright spark, but even that once stable relationship is now starting to fray at the edges. A few yards to your left a youthful guard stands outside an electrical goods shop, glowing like a phantom in the streetlight's incandescent halo. A roadside billboard standing high above the derelict buildings and furrowed alleyways advertised a revolutionary brassiere: *Be a Storm in a D-Cup*. Underneath the caption, in stark black and white, a bald-headed black woman with enormous breasts snarled like a lioness.

You ended up at the busy bar on the ground floor of a small hotel on the edge of the city centre. Inside, you ordered a beer and sat on a stool midway down the long bar counter. The television mounted on a wall behind the barmen was set to a news channels. The proletarian revolt taking place in Libya had gone out of control, said the presen-

59

ter. The downtrodden masses were baying for The Brother Leader's blood. There was chaos in all the major cities. Everywhere, protesters massed on the streets and in the public squares. Game Over, declared a placard held aloft by a protestor. Intrigued, you followed the breaking news story for a while. It was strange how the self-immolation of an unemployed Tunisian student had set off full-scale revolts in over half a dozen Arab states. All across North Africa and the Middle East the uprising has become a public event being chronicled by the wonders of modern information technology. It might have taken decades, but the downtrodden masses had finally found a unified voice.

They want an end to tyranny and they want the freedom to choose how they live their lives. In the past, protesters countered the oppressor's teargas and rubber bullets with stones and insults. But in the new rage the weapons of choice are Blogs, Twitter and Facebook. In Libya, The Brother Leader and Guide of the Revolution says in killing his own people he is preserving the law of the land. He blames an unholy alliance of detractors for his country's woes – Islamists, foreigners, drug takers, Al Qaeda and imperialists. And yet you know it is easy to be absolved from a crime committed in the interests of many, just as you know that he who is present at a wrongdoing and does not lift a hand to prevent it is as guilty as the wrongdoers. Hiroshima, Nagasaki, Mai Lai, Stalin's purges, Hitler's pogroms, the French Revolution, the Balkan conflagrations, the genocides of Central Africa and South America – these acts of subterfuge, barbarism and cruelty were perpetrated for the good of nations. You know it has been the way of mankind throughout the ages – the brutalising of the many by the few.

'People in Libya want their freedom,' said an inebriated gentleman sitting next to you on the bar. 'Do you know that between them, Gaddafi, Mubarak and Ben Ali have ruled for a total of hundred years? These dictators should give others a chance. All of us also want the good life.'

You didn't want to get drawn into a political discussion. So you went outside on the terrace. The conversations here centred on football and local politics. A lady dressed in a tight-fitting dress tapped you on the shoulder and asked you to buy her a drink. It was Sophie, one of the names Helen had unearthed from your cell phone directory. After the bar closed you didn't want to go back to your flat. You knew Helen would still be awake, seething with her prenatal anger. So you reluctantly accompanied Sophie to her lodgings, a room in a derelict block of flats in a seedy part of the Avenues. The block where she lived – Le Chateau Noir – used to be one of the most exclusive addresses in the Avenues before Independence. Now the residents lived in perpetual darkness, like Stone Age cave dwellers, and hung their clothes out to dry on the congested balconies.

Two years before you met Helen you went out with Sophie. She had a good secretarial job with a freight company near where you worked and was studying for a diploma in marketing. Early on in the relationship, her edgy hyperactivity made you suspect she took other intoxicants besides alcohol. But at the time you were not bothered, assuming that was just the way she was. She stayed with an elder sister on the eastern edge of Robert Mugabe Avenue but spent most weekends at your cramped bedsitter on the edge of the city centre.

Sophie was a welcome interlude in your life. You were tired of your nomadic and perfunctory lifestyle and so desperately wanted to make the relationship work. She made you delicious curries for Sunday lunch and in the afternoons you would drive her in your battered Toyota March to the downtown flea markets to buy the pirated DVDs that you often watched all night. You wanted to believe that in her you had finally found the stabilising anchor that would put your life on an even keel. But your love nest was soon girdled with thorns.

Sophie had a gut-wrenching miscarriage six months into the relationship. After that she became a tormented woman. She became tantrum-prone, going into deep sulks at the slightest provocation until you started to avoid her. It must have been around that time that her partiality for *dagga* blossomed into the full-blown addiction that would eventually prove so tragic.

Whenever you had a row, you would go out alone and come back late to allow time for her fury to dissipate. You tried to placate her by telling her that she was only twenty-two, that she was young, healthy and had many child-bearing years in front of her. But she would have none of it. You knew what it had meant to her to have the baby because you had seen the fluffy baby things she had made. And you were aware of the hours she had spent compiling a list of exotic names from her friends who sometimes came to visit. She said when the baby was born she would put all the names in a hat and pick out one.

It was after her miscarriage that your life together became an illusion, a game of intricate deceptions. And as the walls of your imperfect world tumbled around you, you would lie on the extremities of the bed divided by the cold space of your growing alienation – never quite asleep, never quite awake. You often thought about leaving, but to leave one must have somewhere to go to. You did not want to end up alone, having long discovered that the pain of isolation is the worst pain of all.

One day, following yet another argument, you finally decided to move on with your life on what you hoped would be a fresh journey of discovery. You had finally realised you could not sow the seeds of love on a bed of thorns. As Uncle Gideon often told you, '*chitsva chiri murutsoka*,' – new possibilities come out of new ventures. Life has no absolutes, he often said, only infinite possibilities. You eventually left Sophie the night you took her to the hospital and sat in the freezing casualty reception as doctors battled to contain the massive drug overdose she had taken. Now, four years later, you were going through the same bitter experiences with Helen.

✥

The entrance hallway of Le Chateau Noir was dark and stuffy and smelt of old vomit. There was a faded election poster next to the stairwell, the candidate's face reduced to a ghostly outline smeared with overlapping insults. There was more crude graffiti on the stairwell: *We Want Leaders, Not Rulers*. The lift was out of order, so you had to use the stairs. Her room was up on the third floor, a tiny cubicle with a blackened out square window next to a mirror smudged with old lipstick. Through the half-opened window you could see a grey mist swirling in the distance. Below the buildings, cars scrambled like confused insects in the hazy night smog.

The room smelt of paraffin, sweat and old things. Whitney Houston crooned a sleepy ballad from an unseen radio. Every corner of the room spoke volumes about Sophie's disordered lifestyle. Above the headboard was a composite poster of New York City – smooth-skinned skyscrapers, Grand Central Station, Brooklyn Bridge and the Statue of Liberty dissolving in a sulphurous winter mist. Next to the poster was a picture torn out of a glossy magazine – a cadaverous long-limbed European model advertising an expensive brand of lingerie. You both stood awkwardly in the middle of the room.

'Are you married now?'

'Yes...'

'Where is she?'

'She's at home.'

'You had an argument with her?'

'How do you know that?'

'I just know. You can call it woman's intuition.'

'I see.'

'Was the argument about that?'

'Let's not talk about it.'

'Okay.'

Dejected, you sat on the edge of the bed. You noticed how sparsely furnished the room was – a naked light bulb stained with old cockroach droppings in the middle of the ceiling, a red-covered copy of the Salvation Army hymn book on a side table, an old poster of Celine Dion on the wardrobe door, two rolls of toilet paper and a box of free-issue Ministry of Health condoms next to a grimy primus stove. Unwashed apparel littered the floor – socks, plates, jeans, T-shirts – the incidental bric-a-brac of a chaotic life. She sat on the floor next to the television. She fiddled with the controls of the old TV until a blurry picture appeared. It was a late news programme. In Libya, The Brother Leader's son was outlining the options available to his embattled family.

'Option One… We live and die in Libya. Option Two… We live and die in Libya. Option Three… We live and die in Libya…'

Sophie slowly disrobed, revealing a frightfully emaciated body. She sat next to you. You recoiled at the smell of her breath. She put her hand across your thigh.

'You don't have to go back to your flat tonight...'

She started to unbutton your shirt. On the television news, The Brother Leader and Guide of the Revolution has declared total war on his own people.

'You men and women who love Gaddafi, get out of your houses and attack these rebels in their lairs...'

At that moment the electricity goes, plunging the whole block of flats into an eerie darkness. Seizing your chance, you grab your shoes in one hand, shirt in the other, and bound across the room towards the door. Sophie screams after you.

'YOU CAN GO TO YOUR FLAT IN THE MORNING...'

Running home in the dark, you think of Helen, eight months pregnant and alone in the flat. Then you realise all along it has been you who was at fault. You have always been intolerant, pushy, uncompromising. You now realise that whenever you had an argument, her side of the story was just as important as yours. You realise that to make the marriage work, both of you have to make concessions. Now freed of your demons, you feel a new kind of elation. Your fate, unlike Uncle Gideon's, is not at the mercy of the gods but is firmly in your own hands. Unlike The Brother Leader and Guide of the Revolution, you still have time to make amends, to start afresh. And as you sprint breathlessly across the deserted park, the words of one of the protestors in front of the Libyan embassy in Cairo ring in your ears:

'Freedom without sacrifice is like a mirage in the desert.'

Yes, George, the future is born from the seeds of the present, but it always carries with it the ashes of the past.

The Missing

ISABELLA MATAMBANADZO

The sound of metal rasping through rock filters into the murky end of my dream, nudging at scenes I cannot remember well. It's a familiar dream. We are together, my grandmother and I.

Her bedroom provides the space. On her windowsill is a neatly drawn line of uneven jars, cloudy water filtering the late afternoon sun in a rainbow that inverts itself as I rock up and down on the soles of my feet. I stick out my tongue and see its pink reflection. Some of my friends at school have skin the same colour, though we never talk about it. The tip of my tongue swims through the rainbow, dissolving in the strips of yellow, blue, violet; swallowed by the green, orange and red. As the small waves of the water in the jar try to catch it, I pull it back sharply with a plop that sounds like a pebble falling into a stream.

So I think of my younger brother. I wonder where he is and if he made it through. The more I try not to think of these things, the more they snare on the edge of my mind. My brother is flicking stones into the puddles around my grandmother's house, which formed after a storm, like tiny oceans protecting an island.

He's a cheeky boy, my brother, and my grandmother will smack his bottom with a switch from a peach tree. Once because he broke one of her windows playing cricket with a length of driftwood. He was talking to himself, providing a running commentary on his game and batting rather high against the heavy green mangoes that hung low.

'This is the very best cricket we have seen from Viv Richards,' he said in his best West Indian accent, stepping into her special trees. 'It looks as if he's going to break all the world records.' My brother paced out the length of the pitch reaching for the juiciest fruit. He did not see her turn the corner.

This bit is not in my dream. I promise you it's real life. My brother howled and tried to punch her as he'd seen men do on television when we watched wrestling matches. But my grandmother just laughed and held him at a distance with her long arms. His yelping stopped almost as soon as he'd started, distracted by the multiple legs of a *zongororo*.

The water from my grandmother's well is very hard, so it never quite dampens your thirst. I'm not allowed to play near the well. She has put a small fence around it just to make sure. She tells me that the river brings water to her well. We argue about this because I know the river does not have legs. She thinks I'm foolish, my grandmother, telling me that the river in which we swim brings water to her well. I know better.

In my dream, my grandmother's glass jars are filled with leaves from her most beloved flowers. Half full if you put the plant in. Half empty if you pick it up. She does not grow plants from seeds, my grandmother. The grown-ups call her Granny Green Fingers and are forever bringing her stalks to plant in her jars for them. As I go about the garden with her she will lean and snip at a bush here, or reach up and nip at a shrub there. She knows how to make a clean cut just at the groove, where leaves and branches will sprout. The tender shoots bud quickly, growing roots in spindly tentacles. When it comes to planting, she lets me do it because she says I also have green fingers. I think she is silly because my fingers are brown and become even more so with the mud, especially when I squish the roots into her evenly laid out flower-beds, as neat and tidy as her bedroom. It's hard for me to do this planting business: the roots have lots of little hairs that want to go their own way when I want them to go down, down, down.

66

To the right of her wooden dresser is a collection of black and white photographs, an archive of her life. My favourite one has her standing at my grandfather's shoulder, looking right into the camera. She's wearing a two-piece suit inspired by the trends set by the wife of a far-away president. I giggle when my stubby fingers stain the glass, transforming the pattern on her suit into a mosaic. She's a very serene woman, my grandmother, but I will only learn what that word means when I'm big. Sekuru is more brutish, yet in a delicate way. Big people's words, but I hear them: 'Serene. Brutish,' so I have made them mine now. I adore how they come out of my mouth with so much character. Sometimes, when my brother won't play with me because I refuse to be his bowler, I just play with S. 'Sssssserene. Brutisshhhhh' my granite pebble chalks them into the sand. I never play with the B. It does not feel right.

He sits. There, my brutish, delicate Sekuru, in the place traced by my chubby forefinger. He's starched stiff. Age has made his suit chocolate brown rather than the inky black it was in real life. He strikes a pose of the era in ramrod, upright fashion, his back away from the comfort of the wooden armchair, and he dangles his felt hat below his knee. It's as if he is about to take off on a long journey. His eyes show this intent: he has said his bureaucratic farewells. In my dream, it must be the school holidays, because I'm not wearing my royal blue pinafore with the white lace trim and my feet can enjoy how the sun, a little exhausted from warming the concrete in my grandmother's bedroom, ends the day.

And that is where the fogginess comes in. Where I start to see my grandmother walking alone down an aisle. But our church is not designed that way, with austere tradition and regiment, so I do not understand where she is. Still dreaming, she appears as a youngish bride, but one with a silver crown of hair twinkling between grey and black patches, betraying the need for a touch-up with dye. It is her only act of vanity, colouring her hair a very jet black once a month. That, and perhaps if you consider it carefully, her ever-so-fastidious nature.

❧

The scraping of metal becomes a thud, as a forklift crunches earth and moves rubble aside. 'Can you hear them?' I ask my husband. 'Mmmmm.' He turns over, still holding my thumb with his hand. He's always been like that, sleeping with his hand in mine. 'Do you think we should get up?' I ask. 'Maybe later,' he mumbles through an exaggerated snore designed to keep me quiet.

That's his way. In the years we've been together I've found him a quiet man, who loves tranquility. It was not a quality that first attracted me to him. I misread it for a kind of forlorn dejectedness. The error was mine, but it cost us several years together, while I avoided being with him. But now I know, he is a calming, resolute person, whose feet make the slightest whisper as he walks about the house. I remember asking him once to sing, so that I would know when he was about to arrive. He did not say no but he found another way to announce himself, by gently playing with the keys that always have their home in his pocket; or humming, just under his breath, a tune from his childhood. Those who knew him then say he used to strum songs on a home-made guitar. He made the lead in a rag-tag boy band group growing up. It's something I miss, the chime of his keys in his trouser pocket and his gentle baritone coming from somewhere light within him.

My thoughts have taken me far away. It is the silence that brings me back and the smell of very milky tea leaving a plastic thermos for an enamel cup. 'How many do you think we'll find today?' asks a voice, between slurps.

'I don't know. I've stopped counting,' another familiar voice replies.

'But you kept count?'

'Yes, when I thought we would find them. Now, I take it day by day.' He rubs his stomach, which eases his worry a little. 'Day by day,' he says, getting up.

'We'll find them, Paidamoyo.'

His voice has changed with maturity and I do not recognise it. To me his name, Paidamoyo, is just a coincidence.

కచ

The work of washing is always done by women. They know how to find the smoothest rocks, where the river water is still, so that the fragments do not suffer any further. Their fingers are firm, yet gentle – precise. Just like mine. Women's hands, I think as I turn over feeling the ridges of the lines in my left palm with the forefingers of my right hand. They also know how to lift up their voices in a chorus that everyone, even newcomers, can sing. They have unyeilding patience, just as I was taught to have.

Musandipfure Je-esu
Ndino chemera i-mi
Kana mo kombo-re-ra va–amwe
Mu-sandi-pfur-ure…

❧

There has not been enough funding for the project to acquire all the state-of-the-art equipment for this part of the country. They have reserved the money for the most scientific requirements. So the women load the rubble, which the forklift with its hungry mouth has gouged from the earth's womb, into woven baskets.

In single file, they head to the banks of the river, walking to the rhythm of their chorus. There, they rinse the soil, returning some of it to the river, while keeping the bone to one side, where they have laid old white hessian sacks over the rocks. The sunshine does the drying, while the women take a quiet break. There is no need for conversation. All that needs to be said is laid out before them.

At the lab, a new generation of women with B.Sc. degrees in genetics and modern forensic sciences work through the remains. They match, with the assistance of their cameras and computers, this part to that. A stray tooth finds its way beside a female femur. A lone skull joins a knuckle-bone. This one is male. Bit by bit, the skeleton is pieced together. Finally, a whole person lies on the sterile tables of the laboratory at the Centre for the Families of the Missing. Sometimes, there is a bullet hole in the side of the skull, sometimes not. Relatives, who have spent days waiting, cross-legged in the cool of the trees, fold their mats away. They reach out in polite handshakes of farewell to each other.

'See you tomorrow.' They kick the knots out of their arms and legs.
'If the ancestors so wish it.'

They walk past the low-framed windows designed to enable their audience to observe everything.

In the early years, some understandable suspicion surfaced about the lab at the Centre for the Families of the Missing. It was another ploy designed by the remnants of the military government to conceal the truth. For a while, people had stayed away, wary of a further plot, of the purported reappearance of those they knew had vanished forever. During this time, according to a rumour that had taken firm hold, there was a mirror on the back wall of the lab. This talisman served to send back the lost ghosts of the lost remains. One of the ghosts, with a combination of stubbornness and the magic conjured only by those who have crossed over but not reached their desired destination, had managed to graft itself so as to look just like one of the forensic archaeologists. This ghost wanted to be remembered, and mimicked every gesture the archaeologist made. As she lifted a fragment to examine it under a microscope, so too did the ghost. If she reached for a pen to make notes in her record books, the ghost would follow suit. It became something of a living shadow.

People remembered that the grounds at the Centre began to fill the year it rained, when a woman in her mid-fifties, a khaki envelope tucked safely in the left cup of her bra, was first at the the gate. She reached for it with neither hope, nor anxiety. Her work-worn fingers were steady as she handed it over together with her metal identity card to the woman at a desk marked 'Receiving'. An officious stamp recorded the date in the upper corner of her letter: the first of the day in the Arrivals' tray.

The woman was shown to a durable wooden bench, just inside the foyer of the Centre, where in the moments to follow, a volunteer served the growing group cups of hot coffee, accompanied by thick wedges of brown bread smeared with a fruity jam. They ate and drank in silent trepidation, a little uncertain about what to make of hospitality and orderliness not common in bureaucratic offices. They ate with the sensibility of experience, of never quite knowing how long the wait might be in such an office, or if there would be a 'closed' sign thrust before them at lunchtime. The cups and plates were cleared away on new utility trays just as quickly as they had been put out. A young man then worked the bristles of a long broom over the brick floors sweeping up crumbs.

Just as the people on the bench began to relax, they were called forward to a softly lit room where, one by one, they were handed a neatly wrapped and labeled parcel that they carefully place in the cradle of their extended hands. It was no bigger in size than the bundle a new mother is handed by the maternity nurses. And so as the identical twin sisters who worked at the Centre handed them back their original letters, now marked 'processed' and copies filed in folders tagged 'case closed', they accepted condolences for the loss, and the rumour of the ghost in the mirror disappeared. The woman who had been first strapped the bundle of her adult child's bones onto her back, and trekked slowly homewards.

⤚⤙

I had gone to show my husband where we had buried my grandmother, and later, Sekuru. We had left our son, Paidamoyo, with my mother at our home in the city. It was meant to be a short trip, so we left our daughters with her too; born just several months before, they were identical twins, causing confusion that later in life they would use to befuddle their suitors.

I showed him where the rainbow used to arc after rain. We walked my grandmother's route. I told him of the year she had given tough love to my brother for breaking her window. With him, we reached back into my childhood from the safe distance that our love, discovered as it was in adulthood, gave us.

The mango trees were now exhausted apparitions of their youthful selves. Fat wasps had taken over the knobbly branches of peach trees, arthritic in abandonment.

Over the buzz of the wasps, we heard their gruff voices.

'These city people are sell-outs.'

'Bastard children of opposition louts.'

We never saw their faces. We smelt the kerosene seeping through

71

the pores of the aged brick of the hut. Suddenly, the cobwebs in the thatch hut started smoking, kindling the very old wood and hay in the roof we had talked about renovating. We had no words, either of panic, or of fear. We did not scream. It did not take long for the hut to flare up in a barbeque that reduced everything, including us, to ash. There was no smell of us; the kerosene took care of that.

They kept coming to complete the cremation. Stoking the flames with diesel, petrol and other flammable agents. They even had acid.

'Cook them good and proper.'

'This country belongs to us and no one else.'

'We will show them all that we are the powerful machine of liberation.'

'We must finish them all. All of them.'

⊰◈⊱

The first rain of that year came late, but it was gentle with the scorched earth. We were washed, as ash, into the well. We seeped through the veins in the old rock, a sludgy mixture. Now I understood what my grandmother meant when she said the river brings water to the well. I did that journey, with my beloved husband, but backwards. And now from the banks of the river, we hear the women, packing. The day must be over. Their baskets are lighter and lie on their arms not their heads.

'I guess we can get up tomorrow,' I say to this quiet man of mine, who in death, stood by me. 'If you like.' He is polite, even in the life we now live in the river. Too polite to break my heart with the truth that we will forever be missing.

Shamisos

NoViolet Mkha

'These white creepers? They must be taken out. I want them gone.' Method taps his hoe and watches her hands gesture towards the flowering creeper. Her face is ablaze. Method swallows his surprised question, the words drowning in his throat.

The jasmine is in full bloom, their fragrance reminding him of Shamiso, the girl in 3C1 class at Njube Secondary School. Method wrote love letters to her and slipped them into her TM Hyper plastic bag, careful not to sign his name because he didn't think she would ever look at a boy like him. He calls this lovely creeper Shamiso because it brings back memories.

'We'll put red roses in their place,' his madam smiles. Method forces a smile in return.

'It'll be just perfect, you'll see.' Her voice is suddenly cajoling. Method nods, even though he's sure that roses cannot compare to the beauty of the jasmine in full bloom. Shamisos.

'But these are beautiful too, Madam.' Method speaks quietly when he addresses her because he knows the importance of sounding respectful.

'Are you sure you really want them gone, Madam?'

She nods her head vigorously, placing a finger over her lips as her cellphone is ringing. When she talks to Method she uses simple English, as if she were speaking to a small child, enunciating every word slowly and carefully. With other people she sounds normal, and Method imagines her tongue darting around her mouth, dodging her teeth, with speed and precision.

Now she speaks in English laced with French, which Method studied for three years before the University was forced to close. *Right now. Yes-yes. Hell no, I'm not doing it myself, are you nuts? I fired the Nigerian, they're thieves. I mean things were just disappearing. Yes-yes. And I got rid of the Malawian, they're lazy, you should have seen the garden. No, I'll never employ any South Africans, Jesus! They think just because this is their country they're fucking entitled to everything. Yes-yes. No, in the house I have a Mozambican. An old man. Yes-yes. He has a temper but boy can he cook!* Then she switches to French: *Now I have a new gardener, a Zimbabwean. You too? Well, they're everywhere, like cockroaches. Yes-yes. So far so good. Looks unhappy though, not sure what his story is. I'll have to teach him to smile! Can you imagine!? But he's hardworking. And you should see his head, its like a fucking hammer.*

Method fidgets, wishing he didn't understand this language she's using to gossip about him as if he were invisible. He wonders that her mother did not teach her that one does not talk about people in their presence.

The woman looks up from the phone, meets his gaze, and flashes him a smile. Method beholds her coolly. She shoos him away and points vigorously at the creepers. He grabs his hoe and feels her watching him. He would love to get down on his knees and touch the Shamisos one last time but with her eyes on his back, he starts swinging his hoe.

A single hit and the first Shamiso is lying on the ground. He has no time to pick it up, to examine the damage, because she's somewhere behind him and so he swings, and keeps swinging. He does not want her to think him lazy. In no time he has a carpet of dying flowers around his feet, their fragrance suddenly thick in the air. Method looks toward the main house and sees the Mozambican staring at him through the

74

kitchen window.

He does not know the man's name and he cannot see his face because of the distance between them, but he can tell from the way he's leaning forward that he's puzzled. Method looks away. He hardly knows the Mozambican because he works inside the house, like a woman. Now and then Method will see him taking out the rubbish, hanging clothes on the line, retrieving letters from the postbox.

Once, when the Mozambican was hanging out clothes, he had stopped to talk to Method: 'My wife and children do these things for me back home, do you know that?' Method had shaken his head because it seemed the question was purely rhetorical.

'Yes, you don't know what it means for me to work like this, at my age,' the Mozambican continued, and Method nodded in a show of sympathy.

But still he could not help thinking the old man was being unreasonable; it could not surely be that bad, working in such a nice house: the lush cream carpets, the large TV, the deep sofas, the electrical gadgets. It was the home of Method's dreams – that is, when he made it big in South Africa. Then, his mother would live with him, waking up when she pleased to sit in front of the TV with her legs stretched out in front of her, smiling her brown-toothed smile and saying, 'My son, I am proud of you.'

⊷⊷

'Hey you, Zimbabwean! What do you think you're doing?'

Method looks up at the sound of the brassy voice and finds himself staring at a bloodied kitchen knife. The Mozambican is waving it in his face.

'Are you mad? Can't you see you're killing the flowers?'

'I'm not killing them.' Method feels defensive.

'What's this then, air?' The Mozambican scoops up some wilting blooms and flings them at Method.

'Madam doesn't want them any more.'

'She doesn't want the flowers?' The Mozambican's face knots in confusion.

'No. I mean, yes. She wants to plant roses, red roses instead.' Method is relieved he cannot see her anywhere; he would not want her to hear them talking about her.

'But they're beautiful.' The old man's voice is spent. Method looks at his white apron, clean except for a single red stain, and then at the butcher's knife, and wonders what animal the meat came from.

The Mozambican kneels down and cradles one small blossom in both hands, and Method notices that he's missing two fingers on his left hand – Method looks down embarrassed by the sight of an old man mourning a flower. He's relieved when the man at last stands up and turns to leave, taking the flower with him. Method mumbles an apology, though he does not exactly know what for. He realises that he has spoken in his own language, and assumes the Mozambican would not have understood him.

After the older man has disappeared into the house Method goes back to hacking. He is strangely upset, and can't quite explain why. He glances up to see the woman come out of the house and sit on the garden chair beneath the guava tree. She's still on the phone. He thinks of what she said about him, not knowing he could understand her. If he were at home, he would have grabbed her phone and slapped her with the back of his hand. But he's not at home, and besides, she's not a normal woman.

Method had thought they were sisters at first, the two women who shared the house, but one day, cutting the dense foliage behind the bedroom window, he had seen them sitting on the bed. They'd been arguing, and it was after their bickering had died down that he'd seen, from the posture of their bodies, from the way the one with a man's name, who never wore dresses, from the way that she looked at Madam, that this was not sisterhood.

Method had been stunned, then disgusted, remembering how such a thing did not even have a name in his country, how everybody back there knew that such people were not people, they were worse than pigs and dogs. If he'd been at home, he would have climbed in through the window and beaten them senseless, especially that other one who wore men's clothes. He would have raised the alarm and people would have been happy to drag them out in the open and beat them till they could not scream.

And if he had had a choice, Method would simply have spat in their faces and quit his job, but knowing how hard it was to find employment, he'd stayed. Meanwhile his mother's letters never stopped coming, *Dear Method, this is to tell you we are dying of hunger, My son Method, have you forgotten about us?* He had no choice but to stay and work for these two strange women, but he was always on the lookout, to see what they might do.

But they did not do anything, and nothing happened to him. They greeted him warmly when he came to work, paid him his wages fairly, and on time, made sure he was fed from their kitchen at lunch, and did not overwork him like some of his friends complained their employers did. Despite the fact that Madam occasionally spoke to him like a child, he was alarmed at how well they treated him. This baffled Method; how it was that these two, who were surely worse than animals, treated him as if he counted. He did not know quite when his disgust disappeared, but somehow it did, like a fart in the wind.

Method thinks of them lying close together on the bed; he remembers Mfundisi Gatsheni preaching about such sinners when he was a boy, and how they would burn in hell.

Now that he is older, Method knows there is no hell, knows that hell is here on earth, that hell is the terrible road he travelled to reach this country, that hell is the Limpopo River that he had to cross with his friend D. who never made it out because he could not swim, that hell is in the eyes of his neighbours who have lately been telling all the foreigners to get out of the shanty towns and go back home. This is how Method knows these strange women will not see hell, will not burn, so he wonders instead what it would be like to be in bed with Madam. Would she feel like any other woman? Has she ever been with a man?

Lost in thought he misses his aim and the hoe strikes his big toe. He yells and throws the implement onto the ground, holding his foot in both hands. He does not hear himself cry out, but he is yelling for his

77

mother; where he comes from people yell for their mothers when they're in pain. But it is not Method's mother who comes running, but Madam. She drops her cellphone and runs over to him, putting his wounded foot on her thighs, as she examines it closely.

Method forgets the searing pain in his toe, suddenly ashamed by the sight of his dirty foot on her skirt; its calloused skin, the nails he has neglected to cut, which look like claws, the cracks in his heels. He is so ashamed that he wants to get up and run away but she is holding his foot firmly and tenderly, so tenderly something within him yields. He has not been held like this in a long time, and he likes the feeling so much that he wants to give her his other foot, then his legs, then his thighs, then his torso, then his whole body so she can hold it, hold him. He feels the pain in his toe ebb.

'It doesn't look bad, but you must be careful. How come you're not wearing shoes?' she asks, but he does not answer her, he does not know what to say when she is holding his dirty foot like this.

'Your feet are not too big, I'm sure you and Joe wear the same size.' She puts his foot down and scurries off. He wants her to stay, to call her back, but instead he strokes his bruised toe, which is now slightly swollen and bleeding.

She reappears quickly, carrying a pair of blue sneakers in one hand, a small dish in the other. Over her shoulder, he can see the Mozambican leaning out of the kitchen window, his neck craned. She squats at Method's feet and begins swabbing his toe with some cotton wool; his blood is on her fingers. She dries his toe with a small cloth and applies a yellow ointment, then starts to unravel a roll of bandage.

'Can you wiggle your toe?' she asks. Method does so. She smiles.

'Good, you're lucky you didn't break it, Xolela,' she says, and wraps the toe with a bandage. Method hears the name she calls him by; she has difficulty making the –X sound.

Method wants to tell her that his name is Method; that Xolela is not his real name, but he knows he can't do so. Xolela appears on his South African ID; the picture is his, but the name is not. It was chosen by the tall thug Method paid for the document. An unkempt youth with a scar above his left eye, raking fingers through his long dreadlocks while observing Method with bloodshot eyes.

'Method? As in, what? A way of doing things? *Mara* what kind of name is that?' Method had not known how to answer.

'*Mara* you need a real name. One that makes you belong, y'understand? From now on you'll be Xolela. Xolela Mabaso!' And, just like that, as if he were picking something discarded on the street, Method acquired his new name, which he now used for all things official.

'There, I've bandaged your toe. Now try and see if you can put it inside the shoe, but please be careful.' Method slides his injured foot inside one sneaker, which fits comfortably. He does not feel any pressure on his toe. He puts on the other sneaker, and then Madam is on her knees, tying his shoelaces. The wide cleft between her small breasts is not far from his face, so he looks away; he does not want to be caught doing anything wrong.

But she's too busy fussing over him, telling him about the importance of being careful and soon Method begins to feel as if she were talking to him like a child, and he's overcome by a sudden feeling of annoyance.

'I have to go now,' Method announces, and stands up. He does not drop his voice and, picking up his hoe, does not look to see if she is surprised that he does not thank her. Nor does he look up when he hears her on the phone again, but he knows, from the sound of her voice, that she is talking to the other one, the one whose shoes he's now wearing. She's telling her what happened, what she did for Xolela, the gift of the sneakers. Method swings his hoe angrily; he is blind to the Shamisos now, blind to their beauty. He hears her laughter explode and he swings and hacks to the sound, hacks like a madman.

᳁᳁

The sun is sinking by the time Method gets home to Eden Park. Shacks surround him like hands encircling a throat, swallowing every inch of visible ground – sheets and sheets of corrugated metal stretching as far as the eye can see. Method finds the settlement tolerable in the sunset-tinted sky; there is no need to avert his eyes as he does when he's at work; the growing darkness hides the puddles of murky water, the dirt, the armies of flies, the shit, the junk, the queues for water.

He picks his way through the narrow paths, past the Angolan quarter, the Mozambican quarter, the Nigerian quarter, the Malawian quarter; to walk through the settlement is to travel across borders, in and out of different countries. Method does not greet the people he meets. The journey to South Africa, to Eden Park, is a trying one, so the foreign settlement dwellers regard each other with unspoken understanding because they know what has been endured. First, years of gathering courage, followed by painful partings and days or weeks on the roads crammed in the back of poorly ventilated trucks. Crocodile-infested rivers are fearfully crossed and hungry animals evaded in order to squeeze through barbed-wire border fences while fleeing border agents.

In recent weeks the locals have told the settlers to leave, to pack their belongings and get back home. Regardless, the foreigners only observe the locals with amusement, shake their heads and smile. Only those who had not endured what they have suffered could open their mouths and say, GO BACK, just like that, Go back, return to your own country – as if their dream was dispensable, forgettable, as if the scars on their bodies and minds counted for nothing?

Method stops outside the Somali tuck shop whose name he cannot read and contemplates entering. Inside, he sees the bent form of the storekeeper straighten up and turn to face the door. He cannot tell if the old man can see him, but he hears him begin to sing. Method does not understand the words, but he knows instinctively from the quiver in the old man's voice, that he is singing of his homeland.

Sometimes the old man will slip the name of his country into his songs, or names of cities that Method can recognise – Mogadishu, Hargeysa, Berbera, Chisimayu, Jamaame. Method stands at the door, the Somali's song filling the room with his forlorn voice until Method feels he cannot breathe from the sadness permeating him through a language he cannot understand. When the old man's voice lifts like smoke, Method feels the need to escape and turns quickly away.

When he passes the South African quarter his body tenses and his stomach knots. Lately, this part of the settlement has felt like walking through a forest of angry gods. There is something in the air, something unspoken; he can feel it even now, and in order to distract himself he tries to think of other things – the Shamisos, now lying in a pit at the corner of Madam's yard, the red roses, which he will plant tomorrow. When Method passes a group of women blocking his path, he moves out of their way because that is what is expected of him. He glances briefly at the group and catches the eye of a tall woman in a white 'I love Africa' T-shirt. In that brief moment he wonders fleetingly if he should acknowledge her with a nod, but her face darkens with a look that causes Method to trip over an abandoned log.

He quickly rights himself and keeps walking, but there is an un-steadiness to his knees. He has been given many looks in this quarter – dirty ones, blank ones, sympathetic ones, annoyed ones. For the most part, he has learned to tolerate those than can be tolerated, and ignore those that should be ignored, but the look this woman gave him is not a look one gives to humans but to flies, ticks, cockroaches, fleas; to a mound of excrement left in the open, one's stomach cringing in disgust, one's skin crawling in revulsion.

Method feels anger, then humiliation, then something nameless. If he were in his own country he would turn and confront the woman; but now he's hurt, wounded, a part of him wishing he were invisible. Breathing evenly, he walks with care, only lifting his eyes once he reaches his own quarters, among his own people. He proceeds to his shack. He could stop by Njabulo's, his neighbour, where he knows that men and women are already congregated to watch videos from home: *Mukadota, Gringo, Kukhulwa Kokuphela, Neria, Paraffin*. Yet, no mat-ter the promise of good fellowship and laughter, Method does not join them. He knows these gatherings always end with men and women peeling off their clothes to show each other their bodies, touch each other's bodies. Their scars give birth to sad memories. Watching videos is a form of forgetting: the 2008 elections, the police with batons, the soldiers with guns, the militia with machetes. Do you remember? But-tocks burned. Limbs broken. Roofs blazing. I remember. Rape – Jesus,

Jesus, Jesus, rape, not one not two but fifteen of them, one after the other. His sister, Sithokozile, why do you think she no longer speaks? Here, this eye, see it's blinded? Hit by a tear-gas cannister on Main Street. This is where the machete cut, under the armpit, touch, don't be afraid, it only hurts a little now; just don't press too hard. Look, this, here, they say, in Njabulo's shack, their scars speaking in painful tongues. This is why Method does not go to watch movies with them; there are certain things from back then that he does not wish to remember.

He takes off his shoes and stands at the door of his shack, and beats them against each other to remove the dust. Satisfied, he retreats inside and holds the sneakers up to the light of a kerosene lamp. The leather is soft in his hands; he can tell they are very expensive shoes, shoes he would never dream of buying. The black laces are streaked with gold. Method turns the shoes over and inspects the heels; there is barely any sign of wear. He holds them to his nose. He does not know what newness smells like any more, but perhaps it is a whiff of newness that he detects. He is suddenly overcome with gratitude, and he hates himself for not thanking Madam properly. Tomorrow, he will thank her, and the next time he sees that other one, he will thank her as well, yes, he must thank Joe.

⊱⊰

After he has eaten a small supper of porridge, Method spreads his blankets on the floor. He reaches for the sack in which he keeps his things and fishes from it another sack, and from the second sack, fishes yet another. He unties the elastic band around the final sack and retrieves a stack of his mother's letters. *My son*, one begins, *Dear Method*, another, *Method*, still another, and another, *My dear son Method*. He straightens the letters one by one and slowly runs his fingers over her slanted writing, imagining his mother's face – her prominent cheekbones, thick lips, the lines of laughter at the corners of her eyes and around her mouth. This is how he remembers her.

Every day, after work, Method takes out these letters, reads and rereads them and then talks to them, pretending he's addressing his

82

mother. Sometimes he even imitates her voice as he imagines what she might say to him.

My son Method, how come you never write? Have you not seen my letters? He speaks, in her slow drawl.

I have seen them mother, in fact I read them everyday. But...

But what Method, but what? He raises his voice as she would, her head leaning forward as if she were here, facing him.

And you have not sent any money Method. Do you think we eat air? Really tell me, do you think we survive on air?

No, Mama.

Then why, Method my son? What sin have I committed against Jehova to deserve this treatment? Method's palms are outstretched on his lap like those of a distressed mother, his fingers slightly curled.

Listen, Mama. Let me explain...

Sometimes Method's conversations with his mother last well into the night because he has so many things to say. But today, he is hopeful. He intends to surprise her now that he has been paid twice. He reaches again in the sack and fishes out a tin of snuff. He unscrews the red cap and retrieves a wad of folded notes. He glances at the door to make sure it is indeed locked, and then begins counting the money – $320 rands. On Sunday, his day off, he will go shopping for his mother.

He will buy her beans, rice, cooking oil, soap, candles, matches, a dress, vaseline, a pair of tennis shoes. His neighbour, Njabulo, ferries goods across the border, and Method has been saving to use these services. He puts his money back in the sacks. The letters, he places under his pillow and he drifts off to sleep, thinking of the letter his mother will write after she receives the package from him. It will say, *My dear son,* it will say, *My dear, dear, beautiful son, I am so proud of you.*

≪≫

Method is awakened by the sound of screaming. He tosses and turns, pulling the thin blanket over his head but he cannot shut the noise out. The settlement is never a quiet place; there are quarrels, parties, scandals, fights. One gets used to such things. Method tells himself he will not get up to see what is happening – tomorrow, he will plant the red roses, weed the lawn, and, possibly knock down the anthill that is threatening to block Madam's gate. It will be a busy day and so he needs his sleep. He lies still and waits for the noise to recede. He knows it will eventually go away, it always does.

But today the noise clings, like skin, the chaos getting louder and louder. The voices throb, and Method can imagine the air outside quivering, and then parting, unable to hold still. Whoever they are, they are moving toward his shack. Then, for the first time, he can actually hear what they are saying, and he knows from their words that it is the locals.

GO! GET OUT!

LEAVE! GO TO YOUR COUNTRIES RIGHT NOW!

YOU STEAL OUR JOBS, GO!

YOU TAKE OUR WOMEN, GO!

GO, GO BACK HOME, GO!

GO GO GO GO GO GO GO!

And then there are the screams of help, so raw, so scared, so desperate. Method props himself on his shoulders and tilts his head toward the wall. He concentrates on the sounds, listens closely to the intonations, trying to gauge the mood. He has never heard anything like this in Eden Park, voices so terrified, so anxious, so frantic, and others, so vicious, scathing, threatening. Method's head reels. What to do? What, exactly, has happened out there? What's going to happen now? He contemplates leaving his house but decides against it. He needs to remain quiet. Yes, that's what he needs to do, sit tight and remain quiet because who knows what he will find when he goes out there?

Method sees a long spear pierce the shack, and with one twist, his door is flung wide open. Outside, the sight makes his stomach turn. A weapon-brandishing crowd. Spears. Machetes. Sticks. Axes. Knives. Knobkerries. Fleeing bodies. Falling bodies. Bloodied bodies. Screams, pleas for mercy; please please please! And the shouting: Go, get out, go back to your countries! Go! Method does not move from underneath his blankets, though people are inside his shack, screaming at him.

First, a machete cuts Method somewhere on the head. Blood gushes

84

from the wound and his blanket is dark with it. More and more weapons rain down on him. The beatings hurt, and Method feels the pain deep in his bones, but he does not cry out. Then he feels something wet and the smell of petrol stings his nose. His heart pounds in terror. He does not know when the match lands on his shirt but suddenly he is on fire.

Burning sears throughout Method's body. He opens his mouth for the first time and howls. He gets up and runs in a big bright blaze toward the door, but now it is barricaded from the outside; they will not let him out. Outside, he hears a woman scream, Xolela! Xolela! And he bangs on the wall of his shack and screams his real name back. He knows he will not come out alive, but he wants to let them know that his name is Method. My name is Method.

When the Moon Stares

CHRISTOPHER MLALAZI

The sound of a car engine in the village has always been a noise that makes people, both adults and children alike, stop whatever they're doing and watch the road, as if a good spirit is about to appear. It's a sound filled with the nostalgic reminder that we're a people filled with hope, and that we are not alone in the world.

But today the sound of the approaching vehicle elicited a different response. Mother grabbed my hand and we fled into the bedroom, where she quickly closed the door and locked it. I sensed the old determination of a woman who is firm on decisions and reassuring to have around.

'Quick, let's push the wardrobe against the door, Rudo!' she cried.

This item, which stood at the far wall, was heavy, but we managed to push it across the small room and lodge it against the door.

Still breathing heavily from the effort, mother said we must hide under the bed, and we crawled underneath it. Then she pulled the blanket over the gap between the bed and the floor. Darkness enfolded us. The sound of the truck had increased to a steady frightening roar, as if it was right outside. Mother's hands were tight around me. We were not talking, but just listening intently. Finally, the sound receded, and died away. Silence descended on the hut again.

Outside I could hear chickens cluck-clucking, and their chicks chirp-ing. The sound of birdsong seemed to have increased in intensity, sug-gesting that the sun was setting.

✎

We seemed to have been under the bed for a very long time. Then I fell asleep. I had a dream. A soldier was carrying a long spliced stick, and in the splice were cut-off hands and the fingers were wriggling like worms, making all kinds of shapes; then the biggest hand, which car-ried a silver ring on its ring finger, beckoned me nearer; all the hands were now crooked at me, all beckoning me to come, and suddenly the hands were mice and they jumped off the stick and clambered over a soldier; he tried to beat them off as one would beat off flies, and then the mice became Sithabile and the other girls who had disappeared all those weeks ago after I'd left them with the soldiers; and now they were all screaming in one long-drawn-out scream.

I woke up with a start. My heart was beating fast. Mother's hands were still tight around me. It was pitch dark under the bed, but I could smell mother's comforting scent, that of wood smoke overlaid with sweat. The scream that had been in my dream was still there, and now it had become a wail, long and drawn out, like a person grieving. It was a woman. Mother's hands grew tighter around me, but it was not she who was wailing. Then, faint and far off, we heard more wailing, which almost sounded like echoes of the first. And then there was this one wail that seemed right outside our hut.

'It's Auntie!' mother said her voice cracking. 'Mwari wangu! What is happening to us?' Mother speaks fluent Ndebele, but when she is tor-mented she reverts to the Shona she learned as a child.

The wail outside had become continuous, whilst the other far-off wails were still there as if accompanying it.

Suddenly mother released me from her embrace, her movement sharp. 'No,' she said, 'this can't go on, or we're all going to become mad.'

She inched herself out from under the bed, and I followed her. The

87

room was now as dark as it had been under the bed, save for a beam of moonlight stretching through the small window by the door, and lending the room a little light. Mother, in a crouch, moved to the window, and I could see the shape of her head outlined against the moonbeam as she peeped outside.

My parent's bedroom has a sharp smell of mothballs, which are put in the wardrobe to protect our clothes from termites. Maybe it was the lack of light, or the sense of gloom that pervaded the room, but the aroma of mothballs seemed very intense at that moment, as if they had been ground with a stone to release their scent.

Suddenly, mother began pushing at the wardrobe with her back. I moved to help her and we pushed together. The wail outside was maddening. The wardrobe screeched as we managed to heave it aside to expose the entrance again. Mother unlocked and opened the door and cautiously we went outside.

A full moon sat in the sky, like a thoughtful eye. The yard was revealed clearly and sharply in the moonlight. The wails still hung around the village, like a choir of witches. There was no one in our yard. Then mother headed for the front gate, and I followed close behind her.

There is a small hillock in front of my home that hides our hut from the road. Tonight it seemed like an upraised warning finger and we walked around it, following a path. On the other side of the hillock are the homes of Uncle Genesis and Uncle Francis. I walked with trepidation because mother had told me that my two uncles and their families were all now dead. But I couldn't imagine them dead. I had never seen a dead person though I had been to homes where wakes for the dead were being held, and have never liked the gloomy atmosphere.

Uncle Genesis's home is on our side of the big road, and Uncle Francis's home is on the other side. When you get off at our bus stop, which is called Dlodlo Bus Stop after our family name, you get off directly in front of Uncle Genesis's home, and then if you walk around it you pass the hillock and get to my home.

As we rounded the hillock, we heard the wailing voice, which I had thought was in our yard when we had been in the bedroom. It was now louder. Other wails still filled the air from around the village. Then we came to the gate of Uncle Genesis's homestead. Beyond the gate was nothing but five round shadows indicating where the huts had once stood.

A figure, lit by the moonlight, was kneeling before one of the dark shadows and what remained of the foundation of a hut in the yard. The wailing was coming from this figure. I felt a cold shiver run through my body.

Mother walked into the yard, and I followed close behind her. A strange scent of roasted meat caught my nose, but I didn't turn my mind to it as I was concentrating on the wailing figure. Before we reached it, we had to skirt the bodies of three dead dogs, Skelemu, Danger, and Basop, which had belonged to Uncle Genesis. One couldn't approach his home without them barking, even if they knew you, and Skelemu had been the most dangerous of them all, just like our dog, Gadi. Now, we would hear their familiar barking no more.

We reached the kneeling figure, and mother stopped behind it. Then the wail became a voice: 'Oh Genesis my brother, Oh Genesis my brother!' The voice kept repeating itself. The smell of roasting meat had become stronger.

It was Auntie. And as my eyes adjusted to the scene I noticed that the foundation of the hut Auntie was kneeling before had once been the bedroom of Uncle Genesis. In the middle of the floor stood a dark mound, like burned sacks piled on top of each other.

'They're all dead, Mamvura,' I heard Auntie's anguished cry. 'Even Francis and his family. What did they do to anybody? Why are they dead now and so painfully like this? Oh they're all gone, *Nkulunkulu wami.*'

Mother gently put her hand on Auntie's shoulder.

'There's nothing we can do now Auntie,' I heard her say. 'They have gone to join our ancestors.'

'Genesis and Francis never did anything to anybody, Mamvura.' Auntie was still wailing, but the sound had diminished. 'They were not dissidents, but just simple parents who were looking after their families

89

and their livestock.'

Still kneeling, she turned and pressed her face into mother's skirt. Mother placed both her hands on Auntie's shoulders. Auntie sniffled wetly, before breaking into a fresh outburst of sobs.

Mother did not say anything, but her hands lay still and warm on Auntie's shoulders. The more distant wailing from the village still echoed around us. I felt a hot lump stick in my throat.

❧

Mother and Auntie have always argued, especially when Auntie has had too much to drink. Sometimes I think they don't like each other, but I could be mistaken. When Auntie is drunk she sometimes says mother and I are rat-eating people, and she says so in a ridiculing voice. When she does this mother never argues back, but just tells her that Shona people do not eat rats, but mice, which are delicious. I still remember one day long back when I was in our maize field with mother and father, and father had caught a mouse in a trap and mother had made a fire and roasted it. We had eaten the mouse right there, all three of us sharing the parts of the tiny animal, and it had been nice-tasting, like roast chicken. I had asked father if we couldn't catch more mice to take them home for supper but he'd laughed and said; 'Do you want Auntie to call us rat-eaters?' I've also sometimes had this dream of walking with my mother across a valley of tall dry grass, and walking with us is a man carrying a long spliced stick with rows of mice on it. One day I told mother about this dream and she said it was not a dream, but that back in Mashava, when I was a child, she used to go with me and her father, my grandfather, hunting for mice in the bush, and the man in the dream was grandfather, who is now deceased.

But now Auntie is pressing her face into mother's skirt, seeking comfort, and mother has her arms around Auntie's shoulders, giving her this comfort. Then I cocked my ear. I could hear the faint sound of a child's cry. I quickly shut it from my mind, thinking that it was a trick of my imagination, for after all this was not an easy day.

'The soldiers came to the clinic and burned it down, too,' Auntie said in a muffled voice, her face still pressed into mother's skirt. 'I'd just left and was hiding in the bushes. Then they ordered the nurses to un-dress and they drove away with all of them quite naked.'

'So much has happened today,' mother was crooning. 'Put it out your mind for now, Auntie.'

Auntie's shoulders heaved, indicating a fresh outburst of sobbing.

Then I heard the faint cry of the baby again. I saw mother's hands freeze on Auntie's back.

'Did you hear that?' Mother suddenly asked.

'Hear what?' Auntie asked, and a hyena laughed in the night, as if in answer. 'You mean the hyena?' Another hyena laugh responded to the first one.

'No,' mother replied. 'I thought I heard the sound of a child crying.'

'I heard it too,' I said. 'At first I thought I was imagining it.'

Then we were all silent. The wails from the village continued, as if they had always been there, just like the moon and the stars. Our ears were cocked for the cry of the child. Mother gently lifted her hands from Auntie's shoulders, and Auntie's face turned into the night and away from mother's skirt. The moonlight fell on her face, sparkling on the tears streaked on her cheeks.

Suddenly, there was a burst of gunfire. It seemed to be all around us, although also far off, but we couldn't see any gun flashes, or the streak of bullets across the sky. Moments later the gunfire died away, and the distant wailing voices had also fallen silent.

Then the cry of the baby came again.

'I can hear the baby now,' Auntie said, standing up.

There was a mortar and a pestle lying next to the ruins of the kitchen. Mother walked over and picked up the pestle and then she walked toward the charred mound in the middle of the hut. The pes-tle was about her height, and as thick as her arm.

I was watching mother in surprise, wondering what she wanted to do. The cry of the child returned again, this time it was unmistakable, but it was hard for me to tell where it was coming from. I saw mother push the pestle into the charred heap, and the pestle sank through the rem-nants of the blaze. Then she tried to lever the pestle up, but it was too heavy for her. Auntie moved towards her, and the two women levered the pestle up, and the charred lump broke where the pestle was inserted into it, and I nearly ran away in fright.

The charred lump was a mass of human bodies, burnt together. I could now see charred limbs, bones shining white in the moonlight, grinning skulls; the smell of roasted meat was very intense. It had come from these bodies. My stomach heaved and I quickly knelt down. Bile came gushing out of my mouth, even though I had last eaten early in the morning, when I'd thought of going to school, when I thought it was a normal day. I heaved again, then spat and looked up at the women through tear-blinded eyes.

Mother and Auntie were attacking the charred lump. They heaved again, and more charred bodies toppled awkwardly over to the side.

Uncle Genesis had two wives and nine children, including Sithabile. This charred mass of bodily remains was all that was left of them. Finally, only one body remained on the floor, prostrate in front of mother and Auntie. This body was not as burnt as the others on top of it had been. Only its legs were burnt and charred up to the knees, but the upper body was still intact. It was Auntie maDube, Uncle Genesis's eldest wife, and also Sithabile's mother. She was lying on a sheet of asbestos. I remembered these sheets. They had stood for a long time against the wall of Uncle Genesis's bedroom and Sithabile had told me that the asbestos sheets would provide the roof of a five-roomed modern house that her father was planning to build one day.

The cry of the child, though muffled, was louder than ever, and it seemed to be coming from underneath maDube's body. Then I saw mother and Auntie lift up the asbestos sheet on which maDube's body lay, and put it to one side. The cry of the baby increased. Auntie maDube had been lying on ten other sheets of asbestos and carefully, one by one, mother and Auntie laid them all to one side. The last two were badly torn and they just shoved the pieces aside, to reveal the floor from which protruded a metal handle. Mother and Auntie both pulled at it and it came up with a trapdoor that had been covered with grime and ashes to reveal a hole in the floor. A blast of fresh screaming resounded from inside it.

I knew about this hole. Uncle Genesis had it dug in his bedroom floor as a safe into which to put his important things, especially money during the time he had his store, to hide them from thieves, Sithabile had told me that. Normally there would be a small table standing over the hole, but it too must have been burnt to cinders along with everything else in the house.

Mother reached down into this hole with both her arms and drew out a baby.

It was screaming. Mother shushed it and then she stepped back towards me. I had remained kneeling all this while not far from where I had puked, but I now stood up, and wiping the tears from my eyes, I looked at the baby in wonderment. It was Gift, Uncle Genesis's lastborn child, and born from his youngest wife, maNgwenya. About a year old, he was dressed in cream wool jumpers that had a matching hat that covered his little head.

'*Mwari wangu,*' mother was saying. She was inspecting the baby. 'He seems not burnt,' she announced. Tears were flowing unchecked down her cheeks.

A hot lump was now sitting in my throat, and threatening to burst.

'But what about under his clothes?' Auntie asked, her cheeks still glistening with tears. Gift was still crying in mother's arms but his cries were diminishing to soft whimpers.

'It's dark and we can't remove them,' mother replied. Then Gift stopped crying. 'But I don't think he has any burns. Otherwise he would still be crying and he would squirm in my arms.'

Mother then removed her breast from her blouse and fed it to Gift, and the baby immediately started suckling hungrily. I have always wondered when the milk will stop coming out of mother's breasts, but of course I have never asked her, not yet, because the wound from the baby she lost two months back is still fresh.

With Gift still suckling, mother dropped down on her knees, and asked us to do so.

We all knelt. The moon still sat in the sky, as if it was worried about

93

what was happening to us. The night was silent, without even a breath of wind, or the trill of crickets.

'*Mwari wedu*,' Mother began praying. She was looking up at the moon, and the moonlight glinted off her tears. 'We thank you *mwari wedu* for keeping your little baby alive in the middle of a fire, and without your kindness this would never have happened. We thank you *mwari wedu* for being our father when we are in need, and we ask that you show us the way to safety so that our children can also live and grow up to be adults. We pray to you *mwari wedu* to look after all the dead. We ask for protection in this dangerous time *mwari wedu*, in the name of the son and the Holy Spirit. Amen.'

Eloquent Notes on a Suicide: Case of the Silent Girl

BLESSING MUSARIRI

4 December 2005 – Chitungwiza General Hospital

```
Docket Number: CH2345-98
Deceased:      Shoraya Mutema
Age:           Sixteen years
Sex:           Female
C.O.D:         Drowning
T.O.D:         Approx. 3 a.m.
Extenuating
Circumstances: Analgesic overdose prior to drowning
Family:        Father - Trynos Mutema
               Mother - Bethsheba Mutema
               Sister - Anastacia Mutema

Investigating Officer: Inspector L. Chawabata
```

This last case left me deeply troubled. In thirty years on this nobly intentioned but often delinquent force I have seen a variety of misadventures and human frailty. I have been astounded, alarmed, amused, angry, highly entertained and yes, troubled, but never as profoundly as this. I am moved to keep my own record of proceedings and deliberations.

On the evening of 10 May 1992, Shoraya Mutema accompanied her father, mother and sister to an evening church service. It was the seventh day of Advent, the second week of rains, which had come late and gave no assurance of remaining. The unspoken promise was of hard times to come.

Shoraya always stood erect, and had received deportment badges at school year after year, not only for her tidy appearance, but for her collected demeanour. It was noted, with concern, by various of her teachers, that 'Shoraya's work is always tidy and well considered but she needs to improve her class participation.' No one at the school would ever be able to testify as to the sound of her voice, not even the choir master who I quote: 'No punishment I meted out could ever get Shoraya to open her mouth and sing. She stood there and followed the words with her eyes but never sang. I noted my concern to the Head.' When asked, the Head said she had taken it up with the girl's parents and they had simply said, 'That's just the way she is.'

I then asked the following questions: Does Shoraya suffer from a speech impediment? Was she born without speech? If not, did she speak as a child and if so, when did she stop and what caused this cessation?

There is no time in the police force to indulge in sedimentary curiosity over a cut and dried case but I took liberties with the time allotted to me for the completion of my duties. I also took liberties with my own time, often returning to the scene of the crime to further question those who would talk to me, those less troubled but more than curious. My own family is grown and gone and my wife knows I have no timetable. We have managed to grow old amiably together despite the occasional skirmish. It is lucky that we are two deliberate people more occupied with the lives of others than in the one we have shared for thirty-two years. We are two lines running smoothly together in the same direction, connected by the vertical adjuncts that compose our four children but never feeling the need ourselves, to connect. We are compatible in our shared acceptance of this fact.

From my notes:

It's a fairly old house in Mabelreign. The yards are not so large that neighbours cannot be heard when they are sitting on their verandahs, or talking too loudly through open windows. The walls are not high and crime is an infrequent visitor. Bougainvillaea hedges are overbearing to their hosts and jacarandas drop purple carpets, inciting conjunctivitis; vintage cars are less for prestige than necessity. It's that kind of place. A place where a girl like Shoraya could live her life undisturbed. In their Peugeot 405, the family came and went without remark, except the one time, a neighbour confided, when they went to Kazaka – Shoraya's father's home, the time the neighbours stopped hearing Shoraya's voice calling for her sister from the house, or for the ice-cream man to stop. She used to talk, they told me, just as much as the younger one. She used to play and laugh.

'We used to ask her the time...' a young girl giggles. She wears the blue and white striped pinafore of their school uniform. 'Just to see if we could make her talk, but she'd just look at us and look away.'

'Anna was always talking, in fact Anna is a chatterbox, which is why it's so funny that Shoraya never said anything. We used to laugh and say that Anna had stolen Shoraya's words, that she talked for both of them. But you know what's really strange? I never once saw Anna talk to Shoraya. Waiting at the school gates to be picked up, if Shoraya saw their car first, no matter where Anna was, she would know it was time to go. No gesture, nothing. She would just know. And if Anna was the one who saw their car first, we'd just see Shoraya pick up her bag and walk to the gate before Anna could fetch her.'

'She never smiled.'

It's a school for children from middle-income families, run by a convent of sisters. The education here is good and the fees are reasonable. The children are very European in their speech and mannerisms but we are all, to varying degrees, products of missionary education; the difference is in our upbringing and our perceived destinations. Mr Mutema is of the same missionary background as myself; boarding hostels with cold showers and stringent rules, a beans, sadza and cabbage diet, books and Bibles first, personal ambition inconceivable. We were one body united in the objective of pious study for the greater good of the spirit. You can see it in his bearing, the stiffness, the stoic acceptance of Divine Will, the adherence to Christian values that is imprinted on his conscience. Amai Mutema's indoctrination was cut short. I see it in her tendency to beseech. She is not wholly invested in the omnipotence of the missionary God; before the frown appeared on her husband's face, she spoke aloud to her ancestors to guide home the spirit of her child. She repented though, and both returned to the distant horizon of bemused grief.

'Your children are not your children, they are the sons and daughters of life's longing for itself. They come through you but are not from you, and though they are with you yet they belong not to you.' Indeed, not one of the prophets from the 'good book', but wise words all the same. The Bible was more a tool of study for me, a rod with which to chastise those morally errant of us sadza- and cabbage-eating hordes and yet, it lies in its own space in a drawer by my bedside, uncorrupted by any other belonging. It is the bastion of my being, the guardian of my trying soul and I read everything around it and leave it to infuse its wisdoms through divine osmosis.

On the crossing over of the seventh into the eighth day of Advent, Shoraya Mutema locked herself in the family bathroom – an inauspicious space with missing tiles, a cracked toilet seat, and a perfectly preserved enamel bathtub – ran the water to a level sufficient to allow for eventual displacement caused by the weight of her body – her lack of class participation was no indication of a lack of intelligence – opened a brown bottle of generic painkillers, removed the cotton wool that kept the white tablets intact in their multitude and swallowed a handful one by one.

The neighbours are prone to gossip, and this one wants to tell me a strange and mystical story about Kazaka. Her uncle's daughter is married to a man who hails from those parts and she has told her a tale about a natural orchard of loquat trees in which a young girl went missing overnight. 'If you ask the younger one, she will tell you, she was there, unless she doesn't remember it. Perhaps she was too young then.' Anyhow, this young girl was picking loquats with her cousins and other village children when she wandered out of sight of her companions. When it was time to return home, the girl's friends called out her name and she did not appear. They called out to no avail. In the end they recruited older relatives to join in the search and all night they thrashed around in the thicket, calling and calling.

An elderly aunt, unmoved by the proceedings, informed them all that it was not unheard of in this copse of trees for a person to disappear only to return in time. She would be unharmed, they were assured. 'Things happen here,' she said, 'everybody knows this. Pray all you want,' she told the father, whose rosary beads lay reassuringly around his neck, 'but this place has its owners who know nothing of the stations of the crosses that you carry.' In the morning the girl returned, exhausted, voice hoarse, saying that she had been able to hear them calling her all night, and that she had been calling back – how come they hadn't heard her? The orchard wasn't exceptionally large, a person could walk around it in less time than it took to plough one furrow of their largest field. How was it she could not find her way back out and how is it they could not find a way back to her? Everyone accepted then that indeed, things did happen for which there was no immediate explanation.

Anastacia is fourteen years of age. Even now, subdued by the loss of her sibling, she rambles on. Shoraya talked to her – I must confess that all the evidence gathered up to that point indicated to me that Shoraya talked to no one. From what I heard all around me, I am left with the very firm impression that Shoraya somehow existed in this world, as part of it, but seamlessly attuned to her own particular vibration; a smooth body of water gliding placidly along a river bed, no ripples appearing on the surface but moving along just the same, causing imperceptible changes in its environment as it goes along. Anastacia tells me Shoraya used to talk to her about *munda weldheni*. 'She said if Adam and Eve in the Garden of Eden, before their sin, had led the perfect life, then surely Heaven would be a no different place than that. Heaven is a perfect garden in which no one has picked the forbidden fruit and there is peace in the hearts of all who reside there. That's where we go when we die.'

I ask her if Shoraya often talked about dying – at this point I have to accept the young girl's claims that she and her sister held deep and meaningful conversations in the absence of all other ears. I'm unwilling to believe that Anastacia also lives in a world entirely of her own creation. She appears perfectly normal, that is, if normal can ever be perfect; who judges and declares perfection? We as human beings are only capable of understanding the standards we set for ourselves and for each other and who is to say we are, any of us, cognisant of exactitude? I digress.

At the Christian Centre, the counsellors tell me, with the aid of a leaflet to reinforce our informal discussion, that a young person who is thinking about suicide might talk about suicide, or death in general; talk about 'going away'; talk about feeling hopeless or feeling guilty and a host of other things, none of which even remotely seem to apply to Shoraya, but one has to establish certain things irrespective of one's pre-drawn conclusions. No one noticed any change in Shoraya's behaviour.

At mass, on the seventh day of Advent, she was as immaculate as usual, in a pink floral smock blouse and a knee-length cotton skirt with a white lace frill along the hem. Her hair was tied down in tidy rows with black wool; she wore no earrings – her ears were not pierced – and on her feet she wore brown leather sandals that her father had bought on a recent trip to Johannesburg.

'Did she seem more devout than usual? Deeper into prayer than normal?'

'Shoraya was a dutiful child. In church she knelt, rose and sat as always, she bowed her head and held her hands together as she always did. Shoraya wasn't prone to sudden changes. Shoraya was as steady as air on a day without wind.' I am astounded that this steadiness did not seem to alarm anyone in Shoraya's family; there is no one in this life who can appear so absent and still be considered present.

'That's just the way she was,' her mother says.

'But she wasn't always like this. What happened to change her? What took away Shoraya's voice?' Amai Mutema won't speak of it. Holding onto her rosary she turns away to light the candle that is usually burning in the window when I visit the house. 'There are many things we can't control. We just have to trust in God. Only He knows.' God may know the answers but in the meantime I will search. I sense an abdication here, a refusal to be held accountable for the lives we have created for ourselves and continue to live long after it is proven to us that the formula has produced an unwanted result. I am not enamoured of this approach to life. There is enough we cannot change without giving up on the things over which we have been granted some authority. God knows, as the popular saying goes, my own children are nowhere near perfect – or what we have come to generally accept as perfect. My wife and I freely admit to their wilful indiscretions and credit their – albeit, rather few – collective achievements and I can say with some happy confidence that even if we didn't always get it right, we never abdicated our positions, even accepting, as we can only accept, what we have become comfortable believing: that our children are not our children, that they have been placed in our custody by an all-knowing God.

I am inclined to ponder a spiritualist notion: I may be Catholic in belief but I'm interdenominational in intellect. At some point in her destiny, Shoraya's spirit came to a crossroads and the path she chose from then on placed her in a waiting room, in which her physical presence merely became a vessel for transcendence to the next level. Yes, I am sometimes deep in this way. We are after all spiritual beings. If this is the case then there need not be any explanation that any of us is required to understand because these things are beyond our plain of existence. But even as I think this, I begin to wonder about more mortal causes. In many cases like this, and particularly in my experience, a

101

child becomes withdrawn when there is abuse in the family, but I am disinclined to believe this, for reasons I can no more put my finger on than I can understand the person that was Shoraya Mutema.

Shoraya Mutema, as the seventh slipped into the eighth day of Advent, removed her clothes, placed them in the clothes hamper and slipped into a bath of body-temperature water. I cannot imagine that she would have wanted to punish herself with the gruelling adjustment required for settling into a cold bath. She strikes me as a sensible girl. In my mind I see her sitting calmly, waiting until the drowsiness gradually came over her, feeling nauseous from the tablets but ruthlessly controlling the urge to expel them – none of this struggle showing on her face. In my mind, she is serene as her eyes close and her slack body slides slowly under the water, until only the top of her head lies dry and untouched – a fontanel to channel the spirit up and onwards. Shoraya Mutema seemed to have no regrets about leaving this world.

'Anastacia says she talked about Heaven and the Garden of Eden,' I tell her father. He is sitting, Bible in his lap, open at Psalms. He had been reading to his wife and daughter before I arrived. I know this psalm – '... I am worn out, Oh Lord; have pity on me! Give me strength; I am completely exhausted and my whole being is deeply troubled. How long, Oh Lord, will you wait to help me?'

'Shoraya stopped speaking at the age of six. If Anastacia says they talked recently, she is mistaken. You must leave us alone now, Inspector. Our daughter took her own life. There's no crime committed here other than that by her own hand. We must pray for her soul. Suicide is a mortal sin.'

'I would like to understand, vaMutema, what it is that led such a quiet and unassuming girl to take her own life. Surely you would like some answers?' He is right though, it is a clear-cut case of suicide. What am I investigating at this point?

'You're simply fascinated by the life Shoraya led. You want to understand her. You want her life to be about what you know. You think we did something to make her the way she is. Perhaps you have heard the rumour of the loquat orchard. You think that maybe she was bewitched or traumatised or a combination of the two.'

When I look at Amai Mutema, I know that I am not alone in my assumptions, but she is quick to conceal her momentary lapse.

'You want Shoraya's silence explained to your satisfaction – do you think that we never tried to understand it too? That we are so backward it did not trouble us? Some things just are the way they are and you must accept them.'

I cannot accept this. The questions are like weeds in my garden of clear thoughts, they are hardy and persistent, popping up with every minute. Did Shoraya ever laugh? What did she enjoy doing? When she was at home where did she sit or lie down, what was her favourite place? Did she watch TV? Listen to the radio? Read? 'Yes, she liked to read,' Anastacia tells me. 'She liked to read the Bible and she liked to watch the news. When she wasn't in the house, she liked to sit under the mango tree over there by the gate.'

'Did she ever tell you what she was thinking about when she sat under the tree?'

Anastacia is a neat child, as well presented as I imagine was Shoraya. Her hair is tied down to her head in neat rows wound through with black thread; and she is wearing a floral blouse and a knee-length skirt with a lace ruffle along the hem, and a pair of leather sandals that her father bought on a trip to Johannesburg, and for a minute I am very confused. I never met Shoraya, but in this instant I imagine that she is standing in front of me. Have I become so obsessed that I am now seeing the dead girl in her sister? An idea I am trained to reject enters my mind and I decide to experiment.

'Shoraya,' I say, 'What do you want to tell me?

5 December 2005 – Chitungwiza General Hospital

Bed Number: 2D
Deceased: Lovemore Chawabata
Age: Seventy-six years
Sex: Male
Occupation: Retired
C.O.D: Stroke
T.O.D: Approx. 3 a.m.
Extenuating
Circumstances: Comatose on arrival.
                  Never regained consiousness.
Next of Kin: Maude Chawabata - wife
                  Benhilda Muromba - daughter
                  Aaron Chawabata - son
                  Silas Chawabata - son
                  Davison Chawabata - son

Attending Physician: Dr Tapfuma Nesango

Danfo Driver

AMBROSE MUSIYIWA

The slogan on the minibus said, *Zvichanaka chete.*

But things did not get better, at least, not for this minibus. Now it was parked outside the house. Permanently. The tyres were flat. The windscreen was cracked and most of the other windows were broken. And various parts had gone missing: here today, gone tomorrow.

But the slogan remained, *Zvichanaka chete.*

Danny was at the steering wheel. He was driving. He had four passengers. Five, if you included Agnes, the conductor. He was plying the City-Chitungwiza route. He had picked up this set of passengers at Makoni Shopping Centre and he was taking them to the city. He negotiated a corner with skill and precision, carefully avoiding a tomato vendor who sat too close to the road.

He hoped they would be able to fill the remaining empty seats as they drew closer to Harare but, even as he hoped, he doubted this would happen. There had been a time when one could survive as an owner-driver but that time was long gone. This much he knew.

There was water, electricity, rent and council tax to pay. The council had already switched off their water because the bill had had not been paid, not for many months. There were also school uniforms, exercise books, pens, pencils and rulers to be purchased.

His mother had not paid school fees this term. So even though he went to school every day, he knew he could not do much learning. Each day started with roll-call. And after that all those who had not paid all or part of their school fees and those who did not have a letter from the headmaster saying they could remain in class, were asked to leave and return only when they brought their school fees with them.

Some stopped going to school altogether. But Danny woke up every morning, put on his shabby school uniform, which was now rather too small for him, and went to school hoping, just hoping, that today would be different and the headmaster would relent and allow him to stay.

Sometimes he was lucky.

Occasionally the teacher forgot to ask those who had not paid their fees to leave the class and Danny got to find out where the others were with their lessons. But because he had missed so many, most of what the teacher said did not make sense to him. He could not ask those who were sitting next to him because if he tried doing so, the teacher would notice him and would punish him for talking in class. Or, which was even worse, the teacher would remember that he had not paid his fees and would call him to the front of the class, give him a rap on the knuckles with the blackboard duster for trying to cheat and send him out of the class.

He would leave. And he would come back the next day.

He had stopped reminding his mother about the school fees because the last time he did so she beat him so badly he thought he would die. She had punched him, and when he fell, she had kicked him and she had kept on kicking him until he passed out and she had left him on the floor.

She was gone for many days.

Danny did not know how long he had lain on the cement floor. It could have been minutes. It could have been hours. It could have been longer. He did not know.

When he woke up, he was in pain. Every part of his body ached. He could not walk. He could not talk.

He did not go to school for a week.

It took him a lot of time to crawl to the toilet when he wanted to relieve himself. Sometimes he was tempted to relieve himself there on the floor of the room he shared with his mother because his body ached so much, but the thought of what his mother would do to him if she returned and found he had messed the floor, stopped him.

He stopped talking to her about money.

When there was no food in the house, he did not complain of hunger and after a time the feeling went away; besides, when she was there, she always managed to feed them a bowl of sadza, and they always left a little bit to have it cold for breakfast.

He started spending more time in the minibus. He would sit at the steering wheel and drive. He wanted to go as far away as possible and never come back.

At first, he was the only one there.

But other children soon joined him. When they started coming, they found him at the steering wheel. That was when he started plying the City-Chitungwiza route.

They tried to get him to allow them to take turns at the steering wheel. They did not succeed.

He had to raise money for rent and council tax. He had to raise money for school fees.

Agnes wanted to be a nurse. The twins, Lameck and Shelton, wanted to be policemen. Nigel wanted to be a teacher. Robert wanted to be a lawyer. And Mike wanted to be a doctor.

'And you, Danny, what do you want to be when you grow up?'

Danny had not really thought about growing up or about what he wanted to do when he was grown up. It was too far away in the future. But when the teacher had asked him the question, he had offered, 'A combi driver.'

'Ah,' the teacher said. 'A *danfo* driver.

'*Manthatu, manthata, mathantam.*'

The teacher must have seen the amusement written on Danny's face because he went on, 'Minibuses or vans that are used to ferry commuters from one place to another are called *danfo* in places like Nigeria. In Kenya, they call them *mathatu*. Here, we call them, *macombi*, plural, *combi*, singular ... Not very original. It's like saying Colgate when you want to say toothpaste ... or Coke when you want to say soft drink ... or Jik when you want to say bleach.'

The teacher had then moved on to the next group.

Danfo driver.

Danny liked the sound of that.

He was a *danfo* driver. He was going to raise money for school fees and food.

Maybe if he managed to do that, his mother would be happier. Maybe then he would not have to share a room with his mother and her visitors whose bodies smelt of sweat and their breath of kachasu. Maybe she would stop beating him up. Maybe he would not have to go to sleep on an empty stomach. Maybe he would move from the bottom of the class back to the top, where he had been before things got so bad.

The Donor's Visit

SEKAI NZENZA

Just after dawn today, Ndodye stood on top of the anthill and woke the whole village up. He was shouting: 'A message to old ladies, widows and orphans! *Chiziviso ku chembere, shirikadzi ne nherera!* Today the donor is coming only for you. Get up and go to Simukai Centre for your food handouts. If you do not get up now, you will die of hunger in your hut.' Ndodye's voice rules the mornings. Voices travel fast before sunrise.

Every day Ndodye stands on top of the anthill near his compound and announces all the village meetings and events. Last week Ndodye shouted that the donor was coming. Chiyevo and I got up early and started the journey to the food distribution meeting. Halfway there we met Sabhuku, the kraal head. Sabhuku said that was not true. There was no donor coming. Ndodye got the days wrong. We turned and went back home. Ndodye has a big voice. He used to be a soldier. Because his rank in the Rhodesian army was very low, he never had a chance to shout and order people to do anything. Now he's found his chance at last: Ndodye is the village crier, neighborhood police officer and ZANU-PF village chairperson.

I say to Chiyevo, Ndodye was drinking *chi*-one-day beer at your mother's house till very late last night. When did he get this message and how do we know it is true that the donor is coming? Chiyevo tells me: 'Last week he called all family heads. Today his message is only for old ladies, widows and orphans. It's a special day for them. Ndodye cannot get the message wrong again.'

We get up and start the long walk to meet the donor. Chiyevo walks in front of me. Chiyevo is my granddaughter, *muzukuru wangu*, one of my late son's daughters. She accompanies me on long journeys like this and helps me carry whatever the donor gives us. This year Chiyevo will be turning eighteen. She only passed two subjects in Form 4 last year. How could she pass? She missed many days of school because we did not have the money for school fees. I sold my goat, her mother sold two chickens and we made enough money for her term fees, books and uniforms. Then the river was in flood for days and days and Chiyevo stayed home. When she went back to school, the teachers were on strike. Teaching has no money, they said. The government is not paying us enough. We are teaching your children only because we are merciful. Chiyevo got her results at the beginning of this year. She passed only two subjects out of eight. Her mother did not know what to do with her anger: 'I wanted you to become a teacher or a nurse. But you failed. You only passed Shona and Religious Knowledge. Where does that take you? What will you do next? You want to be someone's maid? You want to be a second or third wife to a sugar daddy?'

As usual, Chiyevo shrugged her shoulders, smiled and said nothing. Her mother shouted at her. Called her names and said she had wasted her chickens and her goats paying school fees for a dumb and lazy girl. You do not have a brain, her mother said in anger. Your head is full of nothing but water.

Chiyevo cried and I said she should not cry. She was not the only one who did not pass at Simukai Secondary School. Many children failed.

Chiyevo and I stop at the river for a wash. It's still morning but it's already quite hot. Cicadas are singing. They promise good rains, I tell Chiyevo. She laughs and says, '*Mbuya*, last year you said the same thing. Cicadas mean good rains. And did we get good rains? No. Last year we had the worst drought ever.'

Chiyevo is right. Last year was bad. We harvested very little. The donors did not come at all. This is September and our granaries are already empty. The rains will only come at the end of next month – if they come at all.

There were times, *muzukuru*, when we were never hungry. We harvested more than we could eat. Even these forests gave us wild fruits and mushrooms, I tell Chiyevo. She gives me one of those smiles that says: I do not believe you. What do they believe, the young people? You tell them that there was a time we sneaked out at night to feed Mugabe's men, the comrades. We risked being killed by Rhodesian soldiers. During the day war aero planes flew so low that you could see the white soldiers and their helmets. They could have easily thrown a bomb onto our compound and destroyed us all, as they did in some villages. I also tell her that her aunt, my first-born daughter Emma, her husband and two sons were killed one night and thrown inside a cave. Their bodies stayed there, untouched for several years.

'I've heard that story before. Is it really true?'

Truth. How much truth and how many times should we tell them what happened? How much truth should we leave out? Some people say Emma and her family were sell-outs and they got killed by Mugabe's soldiers. Others say they belonged to Sithole and they were killed by Muzorewa's forces. All I know is that they were not killed by white soldiers, because those who were present at the *pungwe* said they did not see any white men. During the liberation war, more than thirty years ago, I lost a daughter, a son-in-law and two grandsons. They were singled out from the crowd and shot dead. In public. All in one night. I will never know who killed them. But what does it matter now? They all died. I can only thank the ancestors for keeping their bones safe so we could give them a proper burial after independence.

Unlike her older sisters and some of her cousins, Chiyevo is a decent girl. She listens to me and takes advice. One day she will be a good woman to someone. Chiyevo goes to church and works in the garden.

111

Every day she comes to help me collect firewood, cook and fetch water from the well. If these were the old days and men were still strong, I would have gone to look for a husband for her. But these days, where would I look? Everywhere all you can see are skinny men. Even those who call themselves bachelors do not look healthy at all. Some of the widowed men are just looking for a younger woman to care for them until AIDS snatches them away, as it does. The only healthy men I have seen are those who work for donors, ZANU-PF, MDC, the churches and the Chinese clothing merchants. Businessmen are also healthy. They drive big cars and they have big stomachs. These men will take Chiyevo as a second or a third wife. But I will not let Chiyevo go with these men. They will treat her well at first until they find another beautiful girl to replace her. I tell Chiyevo that money can buy beautiful women. She should be patient and avoid situations with men that will lead to sex. One day a healthy looking single good man will come along. Chiyevo does not say anything. All she does is listen to me, nod her head and do as I tell her.

In times of plenty, *mumaguta*, Chiyevo is normally fat, beautiful and strong. At present she is skinny. We all are. We are hungry. This is a bad season. When I was her age, I was fat and already married with two children. My father wanted more cattle so he married me off to Va-Mandiya, Chiyevo's grandfather. I was his third and youngest wife. I came to this village before I had my first period. I was not a woman yet. Vahosi, VaMandiya's senior wife made me sleep behind VaMandiya's back to keep him warm. After my first period, I became his wife. He loved me and called me VaNyachide, meaning I was his beloved.

Chiyevo, do not walk so fast. I am not your age, I tell her. She slows down. I used to be a good walker. Once I accompanied my mother from Hwedza to Mazowe for a *bira*, the ancestor-worship ceremony. We passed through Salisbury on foot. Then when the liberation war came, curfew stopped us from going anywhere far. After the war, the number of buses coming here from Harare were so many. But everything changed when white farmers were forced to leave the farms and Tony Blair and George Bush put sanctions on Zimbabwe. Because of that, buses do not come to the village any more due to the shortage of petrol. They also made our money very weak. All the money in my clay pot could not buy me a cooking oil. Then Obama said we can use his money but where do we get it? People say there are no jobs in Harare. That Obama is just like the rest of those Africans who live overseas and forget where they came from. Tony Blair, George Bush and Obama have made life very difficult for us. We have to walk many miles to Simukai Centre to get a bus to Harare. Everything begins and ends at Simukai Centre – ZANU-PF and MDC meetings, burial society, council meetings, agriculture meetings, Chinese herbal-tea sellers and now the donor's visit.

Chiyevo increases her pace again and pulls my hand. 'Mbuya, if we walk like Kamba the tortoise, by the time we get there, the donor will be gone. Look, Sabhuku's two daughters just passed us. They will be way ahead of us in the queue by the time we get to Simukai Centre. Come to think of it, they are not widows, where are they going?'

I will not answer Chiyevo's question about Sabhuku's daughters. Talking while I am walking tires me. The message from Ndodye was an invitation for widows, old ladies and orphans. Sabhuku's daughters should not be going to the donor for food handouts today. But who can stop them? Sabhuku is the kraal head. He writes the names of those who qualify to get food handouts. We all know that Sabhuku's daughters went away to Harare to work as maids. Some years later they came back with five children between them. Who is going to tell the donors that Sabhuku's two daughters are not widows? And his five grandchildren are not orphans? The donors do not know who we are. We do not know who they are. We just know that the donors are merciful white people from overseas. They do not like politics. Every year we get donors with a different name. Most of them say they are Christians. They have plenty of food in their countries and they do not want us to die from hunger. They give us food through their workers – the local donors who live here.

We are at Simukai Centre now. My legs are sore and my back hurts. The donors are already here. So Ndodye was correct. Last time I was here, a year ago, there was one lorry. We waited for a very long time to get one bag of beans per family. One bag of beans. That was all. Today is different. There is a big lorry covered with a tent. Behind the lorry are two trucks. The lorry is full of sacks. Food. There are many people here. People I have not seen since independence! Jakobho, the Anglican pastor from St Peters is here too. We are the same age. He has lost all his teeth and his back is all bent. Madaka, the war veteran who lost his leg when he stepped on a landmine. They gave him an artificial leg and when he is wearing trousers, you cannot even tell that he has one leg. I heard that he married a second wife with his war compensation money. His son is a strong member of the MDC. What a shame to the family that is. MDC did not give us land. Mugabe did. This is why I carry my ZANU-PF card and my *chitupa* tied at the corner of my head scarf.

When we left home this morning, Chiyevo said, '*Mbuya*, you only need your *chitupa*, not your ZANU-PF card.' I told her that you never know when they will ask for the ZANU-PF card. I am always ready with it. She laughed and said, 'Mbuya, both your cards tell lies about who you are. Your date of birth on both cards say you are sixty years old now. That is not possible because my father would have been fifty now if he was still alive. And he was the last of your eight children. You must be seventy-five or seventy-eight. Also the card says your name is Enifa. Your name is Makumbi.'

What does it matter what year I was born? I ask her. Who was writing the time and the day of my birth? Enifa is my Christian English name, given to me when I was baptized as a young girl and I became an Anglican. I kept the same name when Mugabe's men said I should change and support the Catholics during the liberation war. They said Catholics supported the fight for our land. Anglicans did not.

Chiyevo never learns. She leaves home without her ZANU-PF card all the time. Last time some youths at Simukai Centre asked her to produce it. She did not have it so they said she was a Morgan Tsvangirai MDC supporter. It was just luck that Ndodye was getting off the bus when he saw them harassing her. He told them that Chiyevo was from Chimombe kraal and as they very well knew, there is not a single MDC supporter in Chimombe. He, Ndodye, would not allow that to happen. They let Chiyevo go. I keep telling her that she should just keep both cards with her in different pockets. Right pocket for the ZANU-PF card and left pocket for the MDC card. That way she will be safe when youths from either political party ask her for a card.

This food distribution centre is noisy and chaotic. A policeman is shouting: 'We want order. *Chembere* one line! *Shirikadzi* one line! *Nherera* one line!' My legs are burning. It is hot. The donors are standing further away near the cars. Three men and two young women. One white woman. They are talking and laughing while drinking water from bottles. I am thirsty.

'If you do not stand in line, there will be no food distribution to anyone!' shouts the policeman. Someone needs to tell the policeman that the lines are all confused. Who says an old lady cannot be a widow and a widow cannot be an old lady? I belong to both lines. Orphans cannot stand in line on their own unless an adult stands with them. Some adults accompanying orphans are widows and some of them are old ladies. How do we know which line to go to?

The policeman is getting impatient. He is holding a whip. I think he is close to whipping some people into line. Under the *muchakata* tree, all the headmen are having a meeting. One of them goes to speak to the policeman. After listening to the headman for a short while, the policeman changes his orders: 'Everyone must stand according to their kraal!' I am pushed into the Chimombe kraal line together with Sabhuku's two daughters and their five children. Ndodye helps us and within a short time, our line is straight, long and orderly.

We have been standing in line for a long time. Nothing is happening. My back is very sore and my knees are shaking. Chiyevo comes to tell me to go and sit under the shade of a tree. She will stand in line for me. When she gets closer to receiving the food package, she will call me. I rest under the shade and take my snuff. After a while I feel the need to go and pass water. There are Blair toilets here. The rude nurse from the clinic is walking around shouting and telling people to use the public toilets. I have never used public toilets. Never. Who knows what disease you can pick up from those pit toilets? Their smell is worse than a dead skunk. The bush is cleaner than the toilets at Simukai Centre. I disappear behind the bush. The rude nurse sees me. She shouts at me: '*Imi Gogo*, listen, we do not use the bush here!' I ignore her. I am only passing water. Since when did she start telling people what to do with their private waste? That is not her job. She should be inside the clinic giving injections. She is only shouting like this to get some favours from the donors. Maybe she will get free aspirins to sell once the donors leave.

When I come back from the bush, Chiyevo is nowhere to be seen.

'Have you seen Chiyevo?' I ask Ndodye. He is smartly dressed in a blue jacket, brown trousers, a shirt with red and pink flowers, a yellow tie and a big brown hat. On his jacket are several war medals, probably stolen from dead soldiers. He does not stand in line because he is managing security here. Ndodye will get a double food package as reward for his services later on. He tells me that two donor women took Chiyevo away from the line. He points to the direction where he saw them going. To a car parked under a tree a bit further away from all the activity. I go there to ask Chiyevo why she let them take her away. Now I have missed my place in line. They have given her a chair – the type that can be folded up. Chiyevo is drinking water from a bottle. Two young donor women, one white and one African, are talking to her. They are both wearing pants.

'This is my grandmother,' Chiyevo tells them. The white woman smiles at me. She extends her hand for me to shake it. The last time I shook a white woman's hand was Mrs Janet Smith, the wife of the Rhodesian Prime Minister, Ian Smith. That was many years ago, long before independence. It was at the Agricultural Show at The Range. My pumpkin won the number two place in the biggest pumpkin competition in Charter district. Mrs Smith wore gloves to greet us, just like the Anglican missionary women. I shake hands with both donor women, the white one and the African. They have soft hands – hands accustomed to holding a pen, not a hoe.

'*Gogo*, we want to interview your granddaughter for a project we are

116

working on with the youth,' the African one says. 'She will be back in time to get her food handout.' I do not know what she means by a project. I thank them and go back to the line. It has moved much closer to the food lorry. Sabhuku's girls and their children allow me to go in front of them. When my turn comes, a young clerk shouts: 'Enifa! Enifa Bako! Chimombe Kraal.' A boy born only yesterday calling my name as if he is calling a schoolgirl. Ah, how this hunger takes away all respect for age. I get my bag and wait for Chiyevo under the tree. The bag is heavy. Inside is a bottle of cooking oil, a packet of red beans and a big bag of bulger. I like bulger because it is like wheat and a bit like rice. It is easy to cook. In 2008, three years ago, when we were very hungry, bulger saved us. Chiyevo said she read that bulger came from America and it was meant for horses. But what did it matter? It was food. Starving people ate bulger and within a couple of weeks they gained weight. Village women's bottoms became prominent again.

The donor women gave Chiyevo a small plastic bag with something. When I saw the bag, I felt happy; at least Chiyevo had not been interviewed for nothing. Sabhuku's daughters look at her with envy. I do not want them to know what gift Chiyevo got from the donor women. I will wait until we get to the river, then see the special gift. Maybe they gave Chiyevo biscuits, sweets, a packet of powdered milk or even sugar. Or some US dollars. We need some to pay for the grinding mill services. One dollar per twenty-litre bucket of maize. Chiyevo carries my food bag on her head and holds the smaller bag with the gift in her hand. I walk behind her. We stop at the river to rest and drink some water.

Tell me what the donor women wanted, I ask Chiyevo.

'They said they were doing a research, an investigation. They want me to be part of a project to do with measuring the number of girls able to use protection when having sex.'

'Sex with a man? What man? You do not have a man.'

'That is true Mbuya I do not have a man.'

'So, what do you protect?' I ask. I am puzzled. But I wait. I am expecting her to show me something to eat. Or maybe the gift of money.

After all, donor women come here to give.

'They gave me this,' she says. Then she pulls out several plastic tubes from the bag. I recognise the tubes immediately. Condoms. I have seen them at the clinic before. They are disgusting. Chiyevo takes another small packet out of the bag. She opens it and says, 'And this *Mbuya*, is a female condom. You put it inside yourself before meeting a man.' She hands it to me to have a look.

'Chiyevo, you do not even know what a man feels like. So you want to feel a tube first before you feel a man? And how are you going to have a baby if you put that tube inside you? No, I do not want to touch it.'

Chiyevo shrugs and smiles. Then she says, 'In this packet are thirty condoms for the men and in this other one are thirty female condoms. They are all for the study. The donor women want to know the number of girls able to tell men to use condoms. They also want to know the number of girls able to use the female condom. Once a month I am required to tell the sister at the clinic the number of times I use protection and what type of protection I have used. She will write that number against my name. *Mbuya*, the donors said I must be prepared to protect myself when I meet a man. A man can't always be in control of what happens.'

Chiyevo is smiling. Is this Chiyevo talking? I shake my head. I feel anger rising inside me.

'Chiyevo, you disappear from the queue. I stand until my legs and my back hurt so much while you sit in a chair like some educated lady, drinking water from a bottle and talking about sex and condoms with strangers. Do you eat condoms?'

'*Mbuya*, this is just a study. Nothing else.' Chiyevo shrugs her shoulders.

'Instead of asking for sugar, a bar of soap, or just one dollar for the grinding mill, all you do is sit there answering questions about sex. What do you know about sex? Then you walk away with a bag of condoms for men and condoms for women. Can't you see what these women are doing? They hide behind the food truck so they can snatch you from the crowd and give you condoms. They are encouraging you to have sex before you get married.'

Chiyevo shrugs her shoulders again, smiles and says nothing. I say to her, 'Chiyevo, go back to the donor women and tell them we do not have sex before marriage. Tell them condoms are not food. Tell them only those with full stomachs have time to think about sex. Tell them we want food, not sex. Go back now.'

Chiyevo looks at me as if I am mad. I am not mad. Why should the donors visit us and encourage our children to have sex? Even Chiyevo's mother does not tell her anything about sex. I do. It is my job as Chiyevo's grandmother to teach her about sex and marriage. What is the use of age if I cannot teach my grandchildren our culture, *tsika dzedu?* We are hungry, we are poor, but we still have a culture to follow.

Chiyevo walks back. Slowly.

I sit by the river and wait for her. After a very long time, Chiyevo comes back. She is accompanied by Ndodye. And she is still holding on to the packets. 'What happened? Why did you not give them back?' I ask her. She says the donor women were already gone when she got there. Ndodye's smile tells me Chiyevo is lying. 'So what are you going to do with those?' I ask.

I want to grab the packets of condoms from her and throw them into the river. Ndodye speaks with a soft polite voice: 'Mbuya the donors come to give food and they also give us condoms. We need both to stay alive. You cannot stop change. Let her keep the condoms. It is dangerous without protection out there.'

Then Chiyevo nods her head and giggles. '*Mbuya*, I want to keep them,' she says, looking at Ndodye. Everyone says this daughter of my son is beautiful. What they do not know is that her head is full of water. Chiyevo's mother is right: this girl does not have any brains. She listenes to the donors doing a project on her and accepts what they give her. Now she is listening to Ndodye who wants some of those things for himself. Today the donor's visit has given me food. But it has also taken Chiyevo away from me. I cannot tell Chiyevo what to do any more.

Eyes On

FUNGISAYI SASA

do you ever get the feeling that you're being watched
I thought she was one of those saleswomen selling life-insurance.

'Do you ever think about the future? What would happen to your loved ones if you died? Can they manage the costs?'

I was ready to say that life was for living, not for dying, so I didn't need insurance. But the woman kept quiet for a while. I could hear her holding her breath. I didn't say anything.

you are
The phone went dead.

I woke up wondering why women in this country chased after men. Amai always said that there was only one difference between a woman who threw herself at a man and a prostitute: at least a prostitute was paid for her troubles. I never understood Amai's objections; I liked it when women took control. Lathering a woman with compliments, expressing interest and desperately trying to make her feel like a goddess was expensive work. I had to take her out, pay for the meals and tip the waiter so that I didn't look cheap. But England was different. Women actually had equal rights – the right to ask a man out, pay for the meal, drink heavily and sleep with a different man every night, if that was really what they felt like doing. I respected female emancipation in the West. It gave me the freedom to date a woman without having to worry about my bank balance.

do you ever

There was a persistent drizzle last night. It didn't sound like the rain in Zim. I was used to thunderstorms and downpours that soaked the skin in less than a minute. In England, the rain was jittery, nervous, hesitant. It didn't fall with confidence like Baba's hands beating a drum and pushing ancestral rhythms through gyrating bodies. No, the rain here was like a limp handshake. Amai always said the sound of the rain hitting the ground was the soil's song of thanks to the heavens.

I never heard the soil here give thanks.

get the feeling

Nobody did.

A woman with flame-lily red hair bumped into me the other day. Her keys and wallet fell out of her purse. I picked them up for her but she didn't thank me. She simply held my hand, tightly. The heavy scent of her perfume filled my head with jacaranda trees. It was as if I was back home walking down Montagu Avenue. A gentle breeze was blowing and purple raindrops were floating down around me.

I forgot that she was still holding my hand, I didn't let her go. She leaned in close, pressing into me as she whispered into my ear.

you are being watched

Amai warned me not to bring her a white *muroora*, 'If you can't find a good Zimbabwean girl, come back home. I will choose a wife for you.'

i touched you

My mother was still living in a past when women wore nothing but grass skirts and men ran around in loin cloths hunting down their supper. A time when women couldn't choose their husbands, they were simply given to a man selected by their family. I needed to be wanted, I wanted to be chosen. Love was meant to be a choice, instead of an accidental by-product of marriage.

i choose you

A work colleague asked me if Africans still lived in trees. Didn't he realise that his ignorance was offensive? I tried to explain as calmly as possible that we had houses, city centres and traffic lights. I was seething inside.

every time

'But you don't have electricity,' he insisted. I told him that electricity was a thing of the past, Zimbabweans had evolved. We didn't need lights because we were so accustomed to finding our way in the dark.

Idiot.

I didn't tell him that it took me a while to get used to the fact that there were no power-cuts here. I used to cook my supper early in the morning, afraid that by the time I reached home the electricity wouldn't be working.

beautiful black boy

The woman began calling me every day asking the same question.

do you ever get the feeling

My landline would ring at exactly ten o'clock and it would be her – her voice always warm like a morsel of sadza and spicy okra slipping down my throat.

i am watching you

Her persistence forced me to become more aware of my surroundings. I saw a silver Corsa parked opposite my house a week after her first phone call. There was red-haired woman sitting in the driver's seat.

no more loneliness

The same car was parked outside my friend's house when I went to visit him on Saturday.

black boy, no more tears

I began to run out of milk faster than usual ever since she started calling. Perhaps she made me thirsty.

do you know that i was watching you

I went to a club for the first time in my life last year. As tipsy women jostled each other to reach the toilets, the music rumbled like thunder, which made the glasses and bottles at the bar vibrate. Men followed women as they migrated in and out of the toilet, trailed after them onto the dance-floor and tried to feel up any woman who was too drunk to push him away.

in the club that night

Tight skirts and skimpy dresses rode up their thighs as women tried to keep their balance in heels they couldn't walk in while they danced the night away. I tried to talk to some of them, but their eyes were vacant – lost deep in the concentration of trying to look sexy. Nobody wanted to have a real conversation, they only talked with their bodies. I decided to leave.

i kissed you once

As I waited for my taxi outside the nightclub, a woman with flame-lily-red hair stood beside me. The shimmering stars winked seductively and the moon was beaming like a gold-digger who'd just received a platinum engagement ring. I could hear the woman beside me humming softly. From time to time she would look at me and smile.

'Beautiful night,' I said to her. 'Beautiful.'

She carried on humming and turned away. My phone vibrated. As I reached into my pocket to take it out, the woman turned quickly towards me and kissed my lips. I'd never tasted the mouth of a white woman before. My friends had raved about the wondrous mysteries of British women and their willingness to please.

you let me just as you once held my hand in the shopping centre

I was curious so I didn't stop her. She tasted of mangoes from my grandmother's garden – soft and juicy.

your phone kept on ringing as the taxi arrived and you let me go without a word

Nobody wanted to have an actual conversation.

i know that you were too shy to ask for my number ask me for my name

On Thursday, I worked a twelve-hour shift and my head was pounding with hunger. It was after ten and I had to complete my weekly shopping. I didn't have any milk or toilet paper. Tesco was quiet. I liked shopping at night, a welcome break from the screaming mothers and whiny children. As I walked along the aisle of tinned food, I saw a woman with red hair making her way towards me.

i am not letting go of

A lily in flames.

you, remember me

Her skin was almost as pale as an elephant's tusks.

black boy

Ivory on fire.

you have kissed me once before

I also needed kidney beans

i taste you on my tongue even now, you colonised my lips

and pork sausages.

come for the rest of me

Eggs.

i breathe your name can't you see i am here waiting for you to reach out and touch my hand again, pick me

They tasted delicious with buttered toast,

up you are mine for life, my foreign country beautiful black boy i see you, my mouth is your territory

bacon and cheese.

i know you don't have any milk

The woman walked past me, humming a familiar tune that made me think of sucking the skin and flesh of juicy yellow mangoes on moonlit nights kumusha.*

sorry i drank it all

Milk used to last for more than a week in my house.

you took the bus home after work today i was sitting behind you, you were on the phone i couldn't understand what you were saying you weren't speaking in english your deep voice took me back to that day when you kissed me why didn't you talk to me then won't you speak to me now turn black boy, turn around and look at me

I saw a woman with red hair following me today.

ask me my name i am here behind you i should be beside you holding your hand hold me i heard you laugh it sounded like a river tumbling over a short cliff i wanted to be the rocks at the bottom of that cliff kiss me again

She was the same woman I had seen in Tesco's,

you work almost every day no one waits for you at home there's no hot meal for you to eat, an empty house is what you keep going back to, i want you to come home to me teach me how to cook that white stuff that you prepare almost every day, maybe its tasteless but i like it, i am

the same one who sat behind me on the bus almost every day,

empty without you i barely see you when you're at work you don't talk to me but at least you answer all my calls

the same woman I'd seen in the silver Corsa.

you can't be happy without me

We didn't have stalkers in Zim,

my beautiful black boy

just *matsosti*, rapists, murderers, police and the army. *you can't escape me we are meant to be together.* Yesterday, my house smelt of jacaranda trees *i used your toothbrush* and I found strands of red-hair on my pillow, *your home is always neat* on my shirts and on the sofa. *but it needs a woman's touch* There was fat-free yoghurt in my fridge, *my touch.* I know that I didn't buy it. *i have touched you before* I like full fat yoghurt, full-fat milk and double cream. *i will touch you again*

I had to work nights since Monday, today was my last one. I found a full English breakfast in the microwave when I got home. *i have been waiting for you* I hadn't prepared the food *all my life* but it tasted good. *you are coming up the stairs* I needed a shower. *i can tell you are really tired because you're dragging your feet and you don't notice* I will be off for three days, at least I will spend quality time with *me lying here under our duvet* my girlfriend. She kept leaving strands of hair in my bathroom. *it's after six* Her red hair made the white pillow look as if it was on fire. *you are in bed but you're not looking at me i know you're trying to sleep but i want you to…* I could tell she was awake, I tried to ignore her. *turn* Amai always said I shouldn't bring her a white *muroora* but it felt good to be chosen. *turn your eyes on* My flame-lily turn your eyes on me.

African Wife

EMMANUEL SIGAUKE

Whenever we gather at the house of Sisi Saru, a Zimbabwean who has lived in Sacramento for fifteen years, we immediately form two groups – the men sit outside, or recline on couches in the living room arguing about African politics, while the women, most of them professionals, enter the kitchen and begin to cook while they talk about hairstyles, or earrings recently received from Africa; occasionally, the older ones mentor the younger on relationships, work, education. The men don't always simply sit – if it isn't raining, we stand or sit outside, around the barbecue, the younger ones watching the meat, while the older keep the debates raging. Eventually, the women finish cooking and send a child to check if the meat is ready. Then we'll all go inside and eat, the men to one side of the room, the women to the other. It never fails.

Today, however, it drizzled a bit, so most of the men are inside. Only four of us sit in the backyard near a little orange tree, barbecuing. The three men I'm with, a Kenyan who recently got his American citizenship and two Zimbabweans, have each lived in California for ten years. Since I'm the newest and youngest Zimbabwean man in Sacramento, I must watch the grill. I don't have to do this, but it's our tradition from the village: younger men roasted meat while the elders discussed serious matters. It also allows me to do something important, as I don't have a job yet.

These three always lecture me on how to survive in the USA, often reprimanding me for my inexperience in running my family, which consists of my white wife and our as yet unborn daughter. I haven't figured out the best way to relate to my wife, who already tries to control me. I don't allow this. The fact that I'm an immigrant doesn't mean I'm stupid.

My mentors say I'm too new at everything, period. Enias, the Kenyan, insists that my bad judgment began in Zimbabwe; I should've waited to leave the country until I had already gotten admitted by a university. He tells me I could have come on my own, without the help of some woman, but he doesn't understand that she's not just some woman. I fell in love with her first time we met in Chimanimani. Enias laughs when I mention love, and reminds me that there is nothing wrong with marrying just for the green card. I'm not like that.

On the matter of work, the men have suggested I concentrate on applying for vacancies in warehouses and at construction sites. The pay is better than in retail, collections, or customer service. You're a young man, they say, you can do hard labour. Let our friends, meaning the women, start in the softer, more comfortable fields. I always nod to show that I take their advice seriously, even when they tell me to forget about my University of Zimbabwe degree and present myself to employers as a high school graduate, the basic requirement for these jobs. Sorry, I'm not going to work in construction or in a warehouse. I'll use my education to choose the better parts of bad. 'You need to be more practical, my brother,' says Enias. 'No one cares about your BA here.' He pauses as if to let the other men acknowledge his words; then he looks at me with his small, hard eyes. 'What were you thinking of anyway, majoring in English?'

'He's about as unemployable as they can get,' Makombo jokes.

The others laugh, but it's a kind, gentle laughter. Enias, whom I suspect changed his name to a more American-sounding one when he became a citizen, has worked for the California Corrections Department

127

for ten years. He's a supervisor, but he tells me I'm not yet ready for that type of work, and he doubts that I will ever be. He tells me never to reveal to interviewers that I have an English degree since that will just make them laugh.

'They'd laugh?' I ask. 'It's not as if I would be lying.'

'They don't know that you're not lying. And with that accent of yours, no one would believe you.'

'But don't we all have accents?' I'm thinking about Enias' accent, which is worse than mine. 'Even Americans have accents.'

'Yes, we do,' Enias says, 'but when I was African I didn't waste time studying English in college.'

I don't like this Kenyan's tone today. Who does he think he is? I pretend I haven't heard his comment and say, 'I carry my certificates to interviews.'

'And how many interviewers have asked for those?' he asks.

None, but I've only gone to a few. I was even promised calls at some. At a toy store in Arden Fair Mall, the female interviewer asked about Zimbabwe.

'What's it like there?' she said.

'Much as it's like here, except we have fewer cars.' I am aware of the exaggeration, but enjoying – with that familiar ripple of pride for the place I'd left behind – the idea of talking about my country. She smiled continuously.

'I see you did customer service at… oh, Edgars? Is that a department store?'

'Yes, just like Sears, better than Sears.'

'Better, huh?' She looked amazed, her stare full of promise.

Although I lied about having worked at Edgars, I can say that interview was a success. I'm waiting for the call she promised.

'She was making fun of you,' says Makombo, standing up. He enters the house and returns with three bottles of beer. He seems to have forgotten that I drink, too. Or maybe he now thinks the unemployed don't deserve a little beer.

'You can't let them dwell on national origins,' says Simon. 'That's the basis for discrimination.'

'But she seemed genuinely interested,' I say.

'You always see what's not there,' says Enias, lighting a cigarette. 'That's the problem with new immigrants.'

I focus my attention on the barbecue. I open the lid to let the smoke escape. Makombo flips the rib rack and nods satisfactorily at the perfectly browned side.

He works as a nurse at Kaiser Permanente, but he doesn't look as if he likes people; besides, he wouldn't be a nurse back home either, but in California the job pays well, and it was his ticket to America. He's applying for his citizenship and has already recommended that I consider nursing once I stabilise. Nah, not me... We're not all cut out for people care. Eventually I'll return to teaching.

I walked right out of teaching onto a plane. Later, in San Francisco, I called the school from my fiancée's mobile phone and told the headmaster I was resigning. He stuttered in shock, then started yelling into the phone, threatening to report me or something (half the time I couldn't hear what he was saying). He might not have realised where I was, so I told him to check his caller ID; then I remembered that, oh, the rural school phones had no caller ID. I just hung up, much to the amusement of my fiancée, who knew how much I had hated the school. In one of my e-mails, I had told her that Zimbabwe had become unsafe for me, and we speeded up my visa application.

But now I miss teaching, and it may be a long time before I return to it. That would just kill me: teaching is all I've known. I could become whatever I want in America, but I don't have to suffer first for it. I'll go back to teaching one day – I know I will. I refuse to think of myself as a beginner. But the men seem to want everyone to start at the bottom as they did. I'm different.

Enias worked for a long time in warehouses before finding a real job. I'm already tired of hearing about his first night loading a truck. If he thinks his story will inspire me to do as he did, he's dead wrong. These hands are teacher material.

Makombo says construction work was a gym membership that paid

him, although the Sacramento summer heat was unbearable. He con-
soled himself by remembering that he came from a hot area. He comes
from Zaka, one of the hottest places of Zimbabwe, but that dry heat
doesn't compare to the humid Sacramento summers.

Simon worked in construction too during his college years, but the
job he says he enjoyed most was dishwashing. 'Each time I came to
work I felt like those janitors – the sekurus – we had made fun of in
boarding school back home,' he says. 'Servers would come to the back
and just dump dishes in the sink without scraping off the left-overs. To
them I was the invisible man.'

'You have to be visible enough to become invisible,' says Enias, ' but
when you reappear, you'll land your dream job..'

The women too have their stories. Some began in retail and customer service, but most have worked in live-in care. Caring for people
isn't something I imagine doing, even though it sometimes comes with
free accommodation. My wife and I have an apartment already; besides, washing and feeding people is not my idea of humble beginnings.
These men don't know that I already interviewed with Wellspring, a
staffing agency for live-in care. Sisi Saru made the referral for me, so
getting an interview was easy. The interview went well at first, until we
got to the point of experience. I'd never been in that line of work in
Zimbabwe, so you have to lie about your experience, and I told them I
cared for disabled people in Harare, taking them to the park, watching
them, feeding them. I could hear that I didn't sound convincing so I
started to talk about my grandfather.

The interviewer smiled and said, 'How exactly did you care for him?'

I could have told her the truth, that all I had done was hold his stick
while leading him to a small hill to relieve himself, since he'd lost his
sight, but I fibbed boldly: 'My grandfather was mad. Mad and blind.'
Then I realised that she might think that by 'mad' I meant 'angry', so
I added, 'He was crazy, cuckoo.'

Her smile disappeared and she sat up straight. I told her that I missed
my grandfather, but I could tell I'd lost her attention. And when I left,
I knew she wouldn't call me. I didn't really care. I never told Sisi Saru

how the interview went, and, fortunately, she never asked. I haven't mentioned it to my mentors either. That was my very first interview in America; and I never had to interview for my teaching assignments in Zimbabwe.

✧✧

Their stories of struggle and success are encouraging, with their message that we all begin from the bottom, but bottom for me does not mean anyone's butt; I want to start somewhere close to the top.

Relatives back home have already asked why I'm taking so long to send them money. I don't know if they think I enjoy being idle – it's gut-wrenching, and it turns the taste buds of ambition stale. I often wonder why I quit teaching at the first opportunity of a trip to America to be with my soon-to-be wife. She could easily have come to Zimbabwe and we could have married there. But then came this American opportunity and now I'm here... I become dizzy sometimes just thinking of what might or might not have happened, and the reality persists: six months in the USA and I'm still penniless.

✧✧

Last weekend I left Sisi Saru's place motivated. I spent the whole week filling out applications at restaurants, and I was interviewed three times, at Burger King, McDonald's and Taco Bell.

'You actually went to Taco Bell?' Makombo says, leaning forward.

'I passed their aptitude test, so they offered me an interview on the spot. But I liked the Burger King interview best. If I'm given the job I would work at the drive-through window.'

Enias says, 'And you believe they would put your accent on their loudspeaker?'

'That's the position they interviewed me for.'

Simon and Makombo shake their heads, as if to tell me I've completely lost it.

'So what did you tell them?' Enias asks, his mouth twitching.

'Many things,' I say. 'I explained my wife if pregnant and I need a job pronto.'

The men break into laughter. I focus on the grill; I fight to control

131

the fire made furious by the fat. We never ate this much pork in Zimbabwe. In fact, aside to going to Mereki for braai, I never barbecued at home. That's not necessarily true – if by 'home' I mean Harare, yes, I did not barbecue, but in the village, in Mototi, we often roasted goat meat. In fact, I was the slaughterer of goats in our extended family, but these are not things you talk about here. Try telling an American that you used to kill goats that's all you become in their eyes, a goat killer.

They're still laughing, and I don't mind. I even join in; they can't tell if I'm laughing with them at me, or if I'm laughing because I conquered the fire. I will do better with my life in a shorter time than they did when they arrived here. I know I will, which is why I'm laughing loudly now.

When we quieten down, Makombo and Enias excuse themselves and go into the house where the sadza is ready. Since there's still some *nyama* on the grill, I have to remain outside. Simon decides to remain with me. I know he understands my situation better than the others, and he has assumed the role of lead mentor. He continues to chuckle after the other men have left, and I let him enjoy himself at my expense. Then he cuts a piece of meat and throws it in his mouth. It dances on his tongue, while he draws in air to cool it. When the piece settles, he chews it quickly, as if he wants finished before anyone sees him. Then he looks at me hard and says, 'You actually told them you needed a job pronto?'

In fact, I didn't say this at the interview, but I reply, 'Yes,' thinking the old hands have found it so funny; I might as well keep the fire burning… eh?

He cuts another piece of meat and instructs me to do likewise. 'Eat while it's still hot; this is the best part of barbecuing.'

I'm happy to comply. Just after I put the *nyama* into my mouth, he says, 'You better eat all you can while you're here.'

He pauses, as if he shouldn't have said this, and then continues, 'Do you still do the tortilla thing, you and your woman?'

I ignore his question. What's wrong with eating tortillas every day if we choose to? I chew my piece of meat noisily, and look for another. I select a whole sausage this time, too quickly for him to protest. Sausage is what everyone inside is waiting for.

He shakes his head, smiles. 'Better stand behind the tree so no one sees you. The last thing you want is everyone talking about you, the Zimbabwean without a job who eats all the sausages. You know our women.'

I say nothing, finishing the sausage and wondering what he means by 'our women'.

'You don't want to be the subject of everyone's gossip,' he says.

'I don't care. Words don't kill.' I want to add, 'including yours,' but I don't want to burn bridges.

'A reputation as an invader of food is not what you want in these circles.' He peers back to the porch. 'In case you didn't notice, there are a few chicks in there.'

'Some of us are married.'

'Most guys leave Hell as soon as their papers come through,' he says. 'You're not the first one to do this.'

'I'm not doing this just for the papers.'

'Don't tell me you're in love?' He grins. 'You know about Mako, who came here in the 90s and tried to follow this love thing with an American woman, white like yours?'

'Mako is Mako and I'm me.'

'All I'm saying is, don't let this get into your head; get your papers and leave.' He looks at me steadily . 'Don't be the nice guy who'll get screwed.'

I'm honestly confused, and I just stare back at him. I stuff the last morsel of the sausage into my mouth. I chew quietly, slowly, then I lick my fingers, but when he torches me with his eyes (he already told me I act too rural), I grab a paper towel and wipe my hands, and he says, 'Much better. Try a piece of that steak.'

'It doesn't look done. I can still see blood on it.'

'It's not meant to be cooked all the way through. I thought you said there was Ndebele blood in your family?'

'Yes, there is, on my mother's side, but I'm not eating underdone meat.'

'Especially you, the newly married; don't eat overcooked meat.'

He flips the steak over to show its browned side. Then he throws another piece in his mouth and chews rapidly. At this rate, by the time we enter the house, we will already be too full to eat. He calls these the benefits of manning the grill. Eat in such a way that no one notices some pieces are missing.

Shortly afterwards, we cease to indulge ourselves and resettle back to our discussion. Soon we will be joining the others, and once inside, he will be talking about African politics with the other men, and I will sit on the sidelines grinning. Or someone will play Tuku or Dembo music, and no one will bother me with any more questions about my personal life. I'll be enjoying myself, as I'm always asked to show my fresh-from-home dance moves. This country has surely given me the gift of dancing.

'Where's your wife anyway?' he asks.

'At the mall,' I lie. I know she's at home, perhaps snooping through my papers. We argued again this morning and I would rather not see her for some hours. She doesn't like these African gatherings. No, that's not true, she loved them once – she introduced me to them – until we began to fight, and now whenever she argues with me, she's arguing with the whole African continent. I don't want her here anyway. When she's around, I'm so conscious of being with her that I don't enjoy myself.

'How's the marriage thing working out for you?' Simon asks in his tone of ready empathy.

'Right now I'm just focusing on finding a job,' I say. 'With the baby coming, I'll take any job.'

'That, we established already.' His voice is relaxed, as if we've suddenly become the best of buddies, which, I suppose, we are. 'So I see you don't want to talk about your marriage today. That's fine; a man has to learn not to spill the beans to other people.' He nods as if he's in agreement with his own words.

He got that right. I talk when I feel like it.

'Just stay away from that business of the neighbourhood watch,' he says in a lighter tone. 'Educate your woman about the ways of her own people. She also seems not to understand them.' He looks at the meat as if he wants to pluck another piece. 'What were you thinking when you signed up for all that crap, anyway?'

'I wanted to protect America, that's all.'

'Those people would call the police on you the moment you stepped on their streets at night.' He raises his voice. 'That's if they wouldn't shoot you first.'

'Well, that's how we learn, right?'

'Keep learning. Both of you need to learn, if you really plan to spend your life together.'

He helped a lot on the neighbourhood watch issue. My wife had thought I might network better by joining the Folsom Neighbourhood Watch group. She wanted me to gain experience doing something for the neighbourhood. We attended the planning meeting and met new people, who made me feel comfortable. But over the weekend when I was going to be assigned a street, I called Simon and told him about it; I had expected him to congratulate me, but he reprimanded me and scared me by mentioning shootings.

That evening I argued with my wife over the issue. The fight went on for thirty minutes, before I said, 'You and I must live in our own world to think that people have no problems with our marriage.'

'Of course, they have problems with it,' she said. 'Don't you see the looks on their faces everywhere we go?'

'So why are you forcing me into Neighbourhood Watch?'

'No one forced you to do anything, Fati,' she said, moving about in the kitchen. 'It's not like you'll be alone.'

'Actually, I will be alone,' I responded quickly.

'You don't know that,' she said, rolling a cheese tortilla.

'I can even show you my street.' I accepted the tortilla she'd said I couldn't have earlier. 'They sure didn't give me a partner.'

'So then, forget about them!' she said, ending the conversation.

With that, we forgot about networking in Folsom. A few weeks later, we were evicted from our flat for late rent. We now live in a low-income neighbourhood some Africans call 'the ghetto', but it's near National University, and the complex looks new.

'You'll get a job soon enough. Just keep looking,' Simon says. He's slapping his stomach like a drum. It looks full, although we haven't gotten our plates of sadza yet.

'A temp agency promised to call me on Monday if they need me,' I say.

'Of course, they always promise,' he says, his eyes looking behind me. His stiff, no-nonsense lips stretch into a smile. I turn to see what's there, and sure there's something. Who is she and where did she come from? Young, light-complexioned and tall, she walks as if afraid to hurt the lawn. He kisses her on the lips, and I look away. No Zimbabwean man kisses a woman in public. I don't, and my wife is used to it.

I haven't seen this lady before, but she has the familiar features of a Zimbabwean woman. She has brought out a Heineken for her man.

'Here,' she says, handing him the beer. He points at the small three-legged table near the grill and she puts the golden liquid down on it. I beat her to the bottle before it rolls to the edge of the table, which is on a slight incline.

'Oh, thank you so much,' she says, extending her hand. 'Linda, from Ethiopia.'

'Fati, from Zimbabwe.'

'Of course, I would never doubt that you're from where he's from,' she says, indicating Simon with her large eyes.

Why doesn't she just say what she wants to say, that he's dark, and I'm dark, so we both must be from Zimbabwe. There are light people in Zimbabwe too: didn't she see some of them in the house? In fact, we southern Africans, a majority of us, tend to be lighter than, say, West Africans. She's from Ethiopia, fine, they tend to be light, she's light, but that's not the point. She should not just assume that because I'm dark like her man that I'm from Zimbabwe too. What's wrong with her?

I smile and say, 'Nice to meet you.'

She winks at Simon and walks – or whatever she does with that nice body of hers – back into the house.

136

'You should've married an African woman,' Simon says after Linda has entered the house and closed the sliding-glass door.

'She's African,' I say, referring to my wife.

He jerks his head and looks at me like he thinks I'm confused.

'Her soul is,' I add, because one, my wife has told me many times she has an African soul, and two, I want Simon and I to keep talking.

'You must be losing it, Fati,' he says, without laughing. 'There's medication for that, you know.'

I laugh because I think he's funny to insinuate that I'm mentally ill.

'So she thinks she's African too, your wife?' He takes a sausage that has been pushed to the side.

'I know she's African.'

'And in knowing so you...' he stumbles on his words, his upper lip quivering. I don't understand why he is getting so angry. 'African, you say?'

'All the way.' I can sense my own anger building up.

He grabs his beer bottle by the neck and drinks, then his teeth attack the sausage, which he quickly spits out. 'The package says mild.'

'Yes, it's mild,' I say. 'I ate one earlier.'

He examines the remaining piece and puts it back on the griddle; then he looks away and sneezes. It wouldn't be nice to take a half chewed sausage into the house, so I eat it. And, of course, it's mild. What is he talking about?

He empties his bottle and throws it onto a pile of recyclables. The bottle breaks. Simon clenches his teeth and curses. 'So your thick, Bongwi skull actually thinks this white trash of yours is African?' He pauses to catch his breath. 'So then you must think she's also black.'

'Totally!' I say, chewing loudly on the sausage.

'And what does that make you?' His voice rises. 'Let me guess: you're now the white one.'

'No, I'm still black,' I say, my voice quivering. If I want to think that my wife is African, she's African. Nothing he can do about it. I came to this country on my own, and he came here, well, who knows how he arrived in the US? He never talks about his personal matters. 'So why

137

are you all over my business?'

Simon looks at the meat, brightens his face with a smile, as if he's decided not to waste another minute on me, and says, 'At least you're catching on the slang. Keep it up.'

And I will.

I place the meat in an aluminium tray and take it into the house. A few guests are already dancing while others are scattered in the kitchen and living room, sipping drinks. All the meat brought earlier is gone, so when I place the tray on the kitchen counter several people gather around it. I'm not interested in food anymore, so I go to the refrigerator to find a beer.

CPSIA information can be obtained at www.ICGtesting.com
Printed in the USA
BVOW072109021011

272566BV00001B/3/P